PERSON

First published in 1997 by Eagle, an imprint of Inter Publishing Services
Ltd, P O Box 530, Guildford, Surrey GU2 5FH.
This edition published 2000

British Library Cataloguing in Publication Data. A catalogue record for
this book is available from the British Library.

All illustrations by Ruth Fowke.

Printed by APP, Singapore
ISBN No: 0 86347 209 5

PERSONALITY AND PRAYER

Finding and extending the prayer style that suits your personality

Ruth Fowke

eagle
Guildford, Surrey

For Rupert and Naomi,
Jeremy and Oliver.

Contents

Foreword

'Pray as you can, don't try to pray as you can't.' That healing, liberating, hope-filled piece of advice is arguably the most helpful aid to prayer that has ever been given. And that is the message with which this book throbs.

I first conceived the idea of *Prayer and Personality* when the author and her friend and colleague, Dr Pamela Dodson, conducted a Prayer and Personality Conference in Cyprus where I live. The conference was attended by a group of people whose personalities were as mixed and varied as a box of liquorice all-sorts. There were those who loved to pray extempore prayers out loud and those whose normal prayer practice is to pray in complete silence. There were those who normally use candles, crosses and pictures to help them pray and those for whom such symbols are anathema. There were those whose 'way in' to God is cerebral – through Bible study, and those who encounter God most easily through Bible meditation. There were those who hear God speaking through creation and those who hear God through interaction with others and an interface with the world.

Different though each of us was, we all valued the conference enormously. Some found it healing because Ruth and Pam affirmed their preferred way of relating to God. Others found the guilt of years being dealt with as Ruth and Pam made claims like this:

'Prayer is about finding the most suitable rhythm to enable one to develop a meaningful, vibrant relationship with the living God. He has chosen to make us all different from one another. Each of us must find the prayer pattern that is most suited to foster the development of our relationship with the Creator God. He did not make us to be clones of one another!'

Yet others expressed their excitement as they experimented with the kind of prayer exercises that appear in this book.

This was not the first time the correlation between prayer and personality had been underlined for me. Yet I was so impressed by the *way* in which Ruth and Pam shared their insights that I longed that readers of the Exploring Prayer Series should benefit from them.

'Have you ever thought of writing your material in book form?' I asked before they left the island. By way of reply, Ruth handed me a copy of a paper she had once written on the subject. My enthusiasm grew. I sent the article to David Wavre, Managing Director of Eagle Publishing who immediately shared my enthusiasm. He subsequently met with the author and commissioned the book.

When I eventually read Ruth's manuscript, I peppered it with affirming ticks and words like, 'appetising, yes, perceptive, helpful, good, interesting'. Now, as publication day draws near, I find myself rejoicing that through the book, would-be pray-ers might find themselves set free to pray as they can; set free to give up the struggle to pray as they can't; set free, in other words, to develop a relationship with the Living God in their own, unique, God-ordained way.

Joyce Huggett

Coldicote Castle   R.W. Foster

Introduction

For years I struggled along, trying to develop an orderly, well-regulated habit of prayer and of consistent Bible reading which I never seemed able to keep up for long. I would give up for a time, then something would prompt me to make another attempt, and the cycle would repeat itself. In those days I was quite oblivious to the fact that the model then held out to me did not fit easily into either the erratic hours of a junior hospital doctor or of my particular personality make-up.

I was brought up in a family that went to church on special occasions, and when it suited them to do so. The prevailing attitude was 'don't take it too seriously'. Later I remember being very disappointed to learn nothing of personal faith during the confirmation classes taken by our headmistress. They seemed to dwell on rather remote matters. I recall some Old Testament history, and having to learn about the seven deadly sins with their strange-sounding names. None of this seemed to have any relevance to my sheltered life at the time, and it did not meet my need for a relationship with God. A few years later I went for work experience to a Medical Mission in London. There I met people who had a quality that I had never encountered before. I started asking questions, and soon began the relationship with God that I had been seeking for some time.

After I qualified in medicine it was not too difficult to work out that there were ways of safeguarding some time for prayer despite the certainty of uncertain hours. It took much longer for me to realise that erratic hours were not actually the problem. The difficulty was more the limitation of the model held out to me as *the* way, the one and only way, to get down to prayer. It was a long time before I realised that I was doomed to disappointment and frustration if I continued to try and mould my prayer life only on a pattern that was at variance with my nature, the personality structure with which God had endowed me.

The model held out to me over a considerable number of years suited the many people who thrive when they are able to run most of their lives, including their private devotions, in a methodical way to a pre-determined plan. That plan also encouraged everyone to love God with all their *minds*. There is of course nothing wrong with that; what was so partially sighted was the discouragement of the complementary attitude of loving God with all the *heart* as well. Both are needed for a full relationship. We need to understand our relatedness to God, and also to experience it. I just happen to be one of many who flourish better with less routine and more flexibility in life generally, and who respond more quickly and naturally from the heart than from the head. Because of these personality traits, I and others like me do better when we have variety, spontaneity and the feeling approach much of the time in our prayers. This was something never envisaged or encouraged in the model held out to me.

The fault of course was not in the model, but in the fact that it was presented as the *only* way to pray, and to grow spiritually. If it had been put forward as *one* excellent way among several useful approaches then I would perhaps have felt less of a failure. I might have been more ready to experiment earlier in my Christian pilgrimage. Sadly, it was years before I stopped trying to pray solely in a manner that happened to be at variance with my God-given personality. Slowly I began to realise that the most growthful thing for me was to pray most of the time in a more natural way. In time I found a way that was more in harmony with the style in which I lived the rest of my life.

Since then I have discovered that many other people suffer years of false and unnecessary guilt because they seldom manage to pray in the way that they are taught is *'the* right way' to do so. It may not be the 'hands together, eyes shut, hushed voice' of the primary school assembly, but sometimes it is still implied that there is only one way of approaching prayer. That one way will generally be the one that happens to suit the teacher, regardless of whether it also happens to be the 'best fit' for the learner.

Some people assume that their way of prayer is second best if it is not in full accord with how they have been taught is 'the way to do it'. Others actually give up trying to pray at all. When they find themselves unable to sustain prayer in the way that was taught they falsely conclude that 'prayer is not for me'. They become discouraged and gradually give up allowing time and space in which to develop a relationship with God.

There are of course some people who manage from the outset to find a way and style of prayer that really suits them. They happily stick with it for very many years. Others find that their style evolves and changes as the years go by. When they get older and their circumstances change, so their needs, opportunities and interests alter, and their way of prayer quite naturally changes too. Relationship with God is not a static affair.

It is the naturalness of prayer that is important. It has to fit each person and be consistent with their nature. It cannot be an alien pattern into which we struggle to fit. Prayer is a vital part of life and should never be regarded as an awkward add-on extra. Neither is it a dutiful task to be completed before the 'real' business of life is tackled by getting on with the work of the day.

Listening and talking to God, and just being in his presence, are surely activities to look forward to, and to enjoy. We do that best when we are most naturally ourselves.

Prayer is about finding the most suitable rhythm to enable one to develop a meaningful, vibrant relationship with the living God. He has chosen to make us all different from one another. Each of us must find the prayer pattern that is most suited to foster the development of our relationship with the Creator God. He did not make us to be clones of one another!

There are of course common characteristics that enable certain groupings to be recognised and described as 'personality types', but any two people of the same 'type' are quite distinct individuals. Each of us is the product of our genetic make-up and of our own personal history. We are profoundly influenced by the interaction between those genes and that history, and by all those events that have shaped and moulded our reactions.

4

No one way of prayer is better or more acceptable than any other. Some ways come more naturally and easily to particular people than they do to others. Whatever our natural style, we all need to exercise discipline in developing a life of prayer. The discipline required of one personality type is different from that which will be necessary for another. All will need to exercise their particular discipline in order to grow and mature.

There is also a need for each type to find the time and place and manner by which they are most able to give their undivided attention to God. Just as the when, where and how of prayer differs, so does the what — the actual content of the prayer time. What is 'true prayer' for one person may be more of a preparation for prayer, an important preliminary, for someone with a different personality. Aspects of God that draw some people like a magnet tend to leave others unmoved. It is not that God changes, but we do tend to see and respond first to different aspects of God according to our particular personality bias. And we are all biased in one way or another.

Mother Mary Clare, a great lady of prayer, a previous Mother Superior of The Sisters of the Love of God which is a contemplative Anglican order of nuns, wrote

Prayer is essentially . . . a love affair with God, not schemes or techniques or ways of prayer, but the most direct, open approach of each one of us as a person to God our creator, redeemer and sanctifier. . . . We are seeking God himself, not thoughts about him, nor about ourselves in relation to him.[1]

Some people enter into their love affair with God through their senses, worshipping him in his creation in the here and now. They respond with all of themselves in the present moment, and we will consider their focussed approach in chapter two. Other people embark on their love affair along a different route, that of imaginative possibilities rather than present realities. They tend to roam more widely and their musing prayer process may be difficult for others to comprehend. We will look at them in chapter three. Yet others are quite likely to baulk at the very term 'love affair' with all its modern connotations, for they seek God primarily through their minds. We will apply our minds to them in chapter four. For other people that same term may instantly cause a warm and enthusiastic response for they seek God primarily through their hearts. We will devote chapter five to them.

There is a real need for all of us to respect different forms of prayer as being equally valid prayer.

Having learnt first to pray in a way that is consonant with our personalities, we do then need to widen our prayer repertoire. It is important that we grow in our relationship with God. For this to happen we will need to experiment and try other prayer styles. Sometimes we find, often to our surprise, that we are doing so spontaneously at particular stages of life. Whatever our style of prayer, we all need to live out the fruit of that relationship by engaging in God's world and relating to our fellow human beings. Again, we will do so in different ways according to our own personalities.

Jesus was perfect Man, a fully rounded personality. He was able to employ every human characteristic in the appropriate way at the appropriate time and in the most fitting manner. He was acutely aware of the world he lived in, and employed his senses to good effect. In his teaching he used examples from nature, like sparrows and sunsets, field flowers and common trees. He knew all the local customs and spoke about familiar items like yeast (called leaven in those days), salt, light and lampstands. The musing side of his nature, his imagination, showed whenever he drew on his observations and taught in parables, or went beyond the immediate and the obvious.

The thinking side of Jesus becomes apparent on some occasions. He showed the characteristic bluntness when he said so starkly 'You are in error' (Matt 22:29). The more feeling side of his nature comes through in his evident compassion. One example of this is his response to the widow whose only son had just died. We are told 'his heart went out to her' and he restored the young man to life (Luke 7:12–15).

We are called to become like Jesus and develop all these characteristics to the best of our ability. From time to time we must each work at developing those that do not come quite so naturally to us but which are nevertheless all latent within each one us. We will not become fully mature Christians if we stick only with our natural preferences, although that is where it is easiest to begin. From there we need to move on and incorporate some of our less developed capabilities as we begin to relate more fully to our Creator.

There are of course many ways of defining and categorising human personality. They range from the simple, and often humorous, ways so often portrayed by the advertising media, to the lengthy and ponderous ways of research institutes. They extend from such elementary observations as whether a person is a squeezer or a roller of his toothpaste tube, to complex questionnaires covering hundreds of items. In this book we are using the outline of the Myers-Briggs Typology Indicator and the basic concepts of C.J. Jung.

In the delightful account of Jacob's dream at Bethel, 'he saw a stairway resting on the earth, with its top reaching heaven' (Gen 28:12). We all need such stairways and there are many varieties; some of wood, some of steel, and some even of marble. The steps may be rough or smooth, close together or far apart. It is the purpose of this book to try and help people find their own authentic stairway with its two-way traffic, from earth to heaven and from heaven to earth.

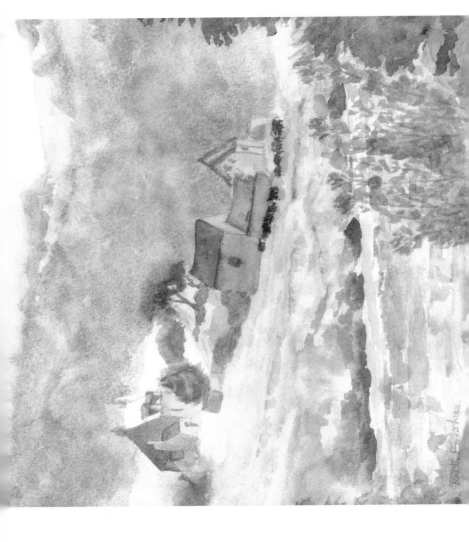

1

Extravert and Introvert Prayer

People tend to develop one of two quite different attitudes towards others and towards the world in which we all live. Some are energised by activity and by interaction with other people. They get a buzz from just being with and talking to others, and seldom want to keep their thoughts or their feelings to themselves. These are the extraverts who need to be active, to have people around them a lot of the time, and who like to talk things through with other people. Others are energised more by the inner world of ideas and of reflecting on the world, rather than by engaging with people and outer activity. It is hard for them to dive straight into anything, they need time for reflection before they are able to speak out or to engage in any enterprise with other people. These are the introverts.

Those two words, extravert and introvert, have a precise meaning in personality typology, and that meaning is somewhat different from the one in current everyday usage. Over the years the word introvert has acquired a rather negative aura. It is now generally taken to denote an attitude that is undesirable, or that is certainly less desirable than that of extraversion. For example, at a recent seminar one man told us that he had mentioned to a colleague that he was coming on the course and he

11

thought the questionnaire would show that he is an introvert. His colleague replied immediately in tones of the utmost consternation 'Oh no, surely not!' as though to be an introvert was the most terrible thing that could possibly befall him.

Throughout this book whenever the words extravert, extraversion, introvert and introversion are used they need to be read with their typological rather than their popular meaning in mind. There is absolutely no implication that either attitude is better than the other. It is of course true that there are situations where the *use* of one attitude is more appropriate than the use of the other. The terms denote only whether a person more readily and easily directs his interest to the world around him, and so gathers his energy there, or whether for the most part his interest is more in the inner world and so he regains his energy more in solitude than in company.

Jesus was clearly able to extravert himself. He went to parties, weddings and funerals. He taught and mingled with the crowds, and at times engaged in spirited repartee with hecklers. He was clearly a people person, but he knew the need for times of introversion also. At times he went into the hills by himself to pray. When his disciples were obviously stressed by people coming and going all the time he invited them to 'Come with me by yourselves to a quiet place and get some rest' (Mark 6:31). He was as at home in a serious one-to-one conversation as he was with the crowds.

Extraverts tend to be always on the go and into everything. They get involved in numerous activities (sometimes simultaneously), for they like to be in the thick of whatever is going on. It is activity that energises them, and not just activity on its own but any form of social activity. It is in interacting with others that they are able to recharge their personal batteries. Conversely, they are generally de-energised by inactivity, by lack of social interaction, and by being on their own for any length of time.

Introverts, on the other hand, tend to come across as relatively more withdrawn from the social scene. They are more likely to be found on the edge of things rather than being at or near the centre of activity. They are in fact drained by constant activity, and especially by incessant interaction with other people. They need time alone. They like to think things through before being required to speak their thoughts out to others, and they need aloneness in order to recharge their personal batteries.

Another characteristic divergence between people with these two very different attitudes lies in their whole manner of communicating. Extraverts never seem to be stuck for words, in fact they actually need to talk themselves into finding out what they are thinking. When they turn to prayer they may have to talk themselves into the silence of listening and responding to God. It is as though they cannot get in touch with their own opinions until they have heard themselves speaking out about the subject. A consequence of this is that they seem to digress out loud, going, as it were, all round the mulberry bush before coming to a conclusion.

However much extraverts may long to talk and exchange views, there are many times and situations when they have to restrain themselves. To be unable to participate, keeping their opinions and reactions to themselves, is likely to be very energy draining for them. When that is the appropriate way to conduct themselves they do not then become introverts, but they do have to learn to introvert themselves.

Introverts, on the other hand, like to think everything through first. Only when they have done so and have formed their opinion will they venture to speak out. They take the line 'I can't possibly speak until I've had time to consider the matter'. When they do speak out they tend to say what they mean, and to mean what they say. All that 'going round the mulberry bush' that is characteristic of extraverts has in fact taken place silently inside themselves. Only the final conclusion is revealed to others. Sometimes they take so long over their silent deliberations, perhaps without giving any indication that they are in fact processing their response, that they may seem to be dismissive or disinterested. They can in fact be very interested, and be very busily considering the matter in their inner world, but they forget to communicate this to the people around.

Their natural tendency is always to hold back, to keep their thoughts and their feelings very much to themselves. Often they do not venture to speak out at all, or at least not until they have been specifically invited to do so. They like plenty of time for reflection, and are often content to be onlookers rather than active participants. Nevertheless there are times and situations when they must extravert themselves. They have to make an effort to participate in what is going on and to talk to those around them. When they do this they do not become extraverts, but they are having to extravert themselves for a time and that is very energy draining for them.

Introverts generally prefer to converse with one or

two trusted friends rather than with a whole crowd of acquaintances. They just cannot cope with several conversations going on at once, although that is a state of affairs that seems to stimulate extraverts. Introverts tend to do their best work, and their best thinking, when they can apply themselves to one thing at a time, and without interruption.

These personality characteristics exert a profound influence on the prayer styles that will be of most help to each of these groups. Unfortunately for the extraverts most writing and teaching on the subject of prayer has been undertaken by introverts. Not unnaturally they have taught and written about the style most helpful to them. Extraverts are generally so busy getting on with the business of living out there in the outer world that they seldom get around to writing, and especially not on the inner life of prayer. This does not mean that they do not engage in it. They pray best in ways that are often quite different from the introvert ways, and there is very little written for them.

Activity, talk and interaction with others are not optional extras for the many people who happen to have a preference for extraversion. These are the vital and indispensable ingredients of life for them. Because such things are necessities and not luxuries, these essential elements must be included in the prayer habits developed by extraverts. They must pray in accordance with their personalities if they are to remain enthusiastic about, and regular in, prayer. Traditionally there seems to have been little to help them.

A number of extraverts who have spoken with me about their prayer times admit to feeling guilty because they tend to pray most easily when they are also doing something else. They have been nurtured with the idea that prayer needs to be engaged in with the same single-minded stillness that is the preferred approach of most introverts. Those are after all the people who have done most of the writing on the subject. Extraverts tend to be multi-activity people. It is therefore quite normal that their regular prayer should be entered into while they are also using their bodies in some active way. For many it is not a distraction but an aid to concentration. Some choose to pray while they walk the dog, or walk to work. Others like to have a more specific prayer place of their own but it is likely to be one where they can move around at least some of the time. Some find a favourite hilltop, or a wood, or a room where they can walk around.

The need for physical activity as a part of prayer has been insufficiently emphasised. Many writers stress how helpful it can be for people to find some special prayer place of their own. Anywhere will do, a particular chair in a corner of one room, a pew in a church, even a cupboard at home, anywhere as long as it is somewhere private where they can be free from external interruptions. Most writers seem to make the assumption that the person who prays will remain static when they get to their chosen place. Richard Foster in his comprehensive book *Prayer*[1] does talk about going outside to shoot a ball into his basketball net each evening while engaged in a specific prayer exercise – a review of the day called the 'examen'. A few people mention dancing as prayer but they seem to be writing for those with a specific interest in that form of movement, rather than acknowledging that physical activity itself can be prayer. It can certainly be incorporated into and become a real help to communion with God.

Very few writers and teachers mention the possibility of praying regularly *and as a matter of choice* while walking or jogging or doing some routine action like trimming hedges and cleaning windows. Many people like to utilise the time on long or familiar drives as prayer time, and some also find benefit in later writing down the result of their reflections in the form of a prayer. The speaking aloud of their prayer as they drive, and the writing down on paper later, are a form of engagement with the external world which is vitally important to them.

Just as extraverts like to talk everyday things out with others so they sometimes prefer to pray aloud with others rather than always on their own. Many find that they are able to spend longer and pray in greater depth, when they are praying with another person, or a small group of people. In congregational worship they often find themselves drawn to responsive prayers, as the regular articulation, the speaking out, helps them to focus.

Because they tend to be active people with a liking for interaction with others, extraverts tend to be very involved in the affairs of their community and their church. Much of their prayer will therefore tend to be the prayer of engaging in their particular activity for others. In fact the prayer of doing can be just as much a valid and fruitful relationship with God as is the more traditional way of the introvert.

The prayer of an introvert, as so much else in their lives, is generally a very private matter. They like to pray alone, and without any interruptions. It takes time for them to disengage from their activities and duties and really concentrate on God. Some do like to pray aloud at times, if they are sure they really are alone, but vocalising their prayer is not as essential for them as it often is for an extravert. They seldom have the need, as many extraverts do, for physical activity to accompany their prayer.

Neither group has a monopoly on communion with God, and both ways have their own particular hazards. The extravert can be so busy doing things in the service of God that he forgets to pay particular attention to the God whom he is serving. The introvert can be so preoccupied with his inner concerns that when trying to pray about them he is liable to forget the God to whom he is praying.

In view of all that has been written in this chapter it is not surprising to learn that there is a tendency for the extravert to relate most easily to the God who is out there, at work in his world. Extraverts will most readily seek a relationship with God Transcendent, who is active in the world, and who surpasses human experience. They may have to work at responding as readily to God who is also immanent, the God who is within, who is part of our human experience and is close to our everyday world. That is of course the aspect of God which most easily appeals to the introvert who will have to work correspondingly hard at realising the vastness and majesty of God Transcendent.

Some Suggestions

If you are an extravert, or want to develop some of the extravert prayer characteristics:

1. Take a prayer walk around your neighbourhood, with friends. Pray for all that is going on (or perhaps that is *not* going on), and for the occupants of the houses that you pass. When you return to base share with the others your thoughts, feelings and insights from the walk.

   - Has God been speaking to you about anything?
   - If so is there any action that you, individually or as a group, need to take; how and when will you take it?

2. Arrange to spend some time walking with friends, stopping off at churches or other places along the way, or after a set amount of time. Read Scripture and pray together.

3. Find some friends willing to go on a Theme Retreat with you.
   Ones such as Painting and Prayer, Calligraphy and Prayer, Embroidery and Prayer, Gardening and Prayer can be found in the pages of the magazine *Vision*.

4. Go on a retreat that is silent for only part of each day, perhaps from the evening meal until after breakfast. Try a preached retreat that also offers the opportunity for individual discussion with a leader. Again, consult the magazine *Vision*; you will be spoilt for choice.

5. Find a Quiet Garden near you that is open specifically to provide a prayer haven. Write to

the Quiet Garden Trust, Stoke Poges, Bucks for information.

6. Arrange to meet regularly, say once a month, with a prayer partner or group; the discipline will enhance your prayer life.

If you are an introvert, or want to develop introvert ways of praying:

1. If you cannot find privacy at home seek out a Quiet House in your area. Some Diocesan Offices now have a list of those whose owners are happy to offer a room for a few hours, and many Retreat Houses offer a room for a day or half-day, when available.

2. Join with one or two others to pray regularly for mutual concerns, and for each other. By meeting and sharing together as prayer twins or triplets, perhaps on a weekly basis, you will build up trust that will enable deeper sharing and encourage you in your prayer.

3. Join a group who regularly practise silent prayer, such as a Julian Meeting. A list of such groups can be obtained from the National Retreat Association, The Central Hall, 256 Bermondsey St, London SE1 3UJ, who also publish the magazine *Vision*.

4. Browse through the Prayer section in any library. As you read, make a note of things you would like to try one day. Copy out for

future use prayers that are especially meaningful to you.

5. Find someone with whom you can share from time to time about your joys and frustrations as you develop your life of prayer.

2

Focussed Prayer

The best example I know of being fully focussed on the job in hand is that of sheepdogs at work. If you have ever seen them out in the hills, at trials, or on TV, in *One Man and His Dog*, then you have probably marvelled at their total preoccupation – they concentrate only on the present moment. They are wholly alert, eyes watching every movement, muscles quivering with readiness, ears pricked to pick up distant commands. Each dog has complete concentration on the task in hand, in the here and now. They respond rapidly to any number of sensory cues.

For them there is no other time scale, they are utterly caught up in the present moment. Some people are rather like that; there really is only one time span for them. The past is gone and the future is yet to come so it is only 'now' that matters. They value the wisdom of experience because that is factual and known, but they do need it to be applied in the present, since for them there is no other operative time. On the whole they are not into dreams and visions for the future, as are those we consider in the next chapter. They are too firmly anchored in the here and now.

They learn about the world through their five bodily senses of sight, hearing, taste, touch and scent. Their senses tend to be very well developed and utilised, with the result that they are generally very observant people.

They prefer to deal with a reality that can be verified and checked, and to apply facts so that they can know where they are. These are the practical folk who notice what is going on around them, and who like to deal with things and people in a direct and immediate way. They are the realists who tend to be so good in a practical crisis. If there is a burst pipe they will go straight for the stopcock and deal with the emergency while others are still vaguely wondering where all the water is coming from.

Detail is very important to such people. They register and respond to such things as scuff marks, or any items that are out of place. Pictures that are not hung quite straight can make them really uncomfortable and they want to put matters right. When one of my friends visits me she can resist the urge for a time but after a while she generally asks if I mind if she puts at least one of my pictures straight. Sometimes I will have noticed a certain crookedness but while it has not bothered me unduly it really fidgets her. Such people like things to be orderly and predictable, and on the whole they like to be orderly in themselves and in whatever activity they undertake.

Their conversation tends to be factual and straightforward, without embellishment. Ask them the time and they will tell you exactly. Seldom will they question why you want to know, or add anything to their very precise answer. At times they can be so concerned with absolute accuracy that they seem to be unable to discriminate between which facts are important and which are irrelevant. For example a host welcoming his guest and asking 'What sort of journey did you have?' probably only wants to know if it was pleasant and straightforward and without major incident. He may be taken aback when, in great detail, he is regaled instead with all sorts of minutiae about roadworks and diversions.

Generally these people like to do things according to specific instructions, commencing at the beginning and working steadily through each step in correct sequence. It is important for them to know 'the right way' to do whatever they undertake, and to be able to follow standard operating procedures correctly. They tend to hold procedure in high regard, and may be relatively low on innovation. They do not like change and if it must come it should, for them, be by slow evolution after due warning and preparation. Maintaining the status quo is important for their well-being, and sameness helps them to function at their best.

These characteristics of precision, exactness and order reflect part of the character of God. They are particularly noticeable in the laws and procedures, the offerings and rituals laid down for the Children of Israel. They emerged from four hundred years of slavery needing to become not just a nation, but a holy nation. It was therefore important for them to have clear guidelines. These are recorded in the latter half of Exodus and in the books of Numbers and Deuteronomy. Of the four Gospel writers, Mark is the only one to mention incidental facts that he observed. For instance, in the story of the feeding of the five thousand he is the only one to mention that the grass was green at the time. For many months it is bleached in the strong sunshine so this fact gives some indication of the time of year when this incredible event occurred.

Jesus showed his powers of acute observation, and his affinity with all his senses, by his many references to daily life going on all around him. He spoke of the wildlife of the hills, and of domestic animals, of wolves and sheep. He used the common things of life to illustrate his teaching: bread and fish, moths and rust, grass and sparrows, salt, light. He drew lessons from such familiar experiences as weddings and funerals, lost coins and burst water mains (well, wineskins actually). At the end of his life on earth he gave recognition of the fact that we are all bodily people, when he quite deliberately and specifically gave us a memorial feast that uses our senses. Every time we take communion or celebrate a mass we are using all our five senses of sight, hearing, touch, taste and scent so that the body can help us to understand and to worship.

Not surprisingly, people who find out about the world and who experience life mainly through their senses, frequently find that their initial contact with God is also mediated through their senses. They find him most easily through his creation, in a tangible, contactable way. Seeing a sunrise, feeling the texture of a pebble, hearing the many sounds all around them, and smelling the earth or the dust after rain, can all lead them to God. Listening to birdsong, music or the laughter of children, can awaken and instruct their soul.

Often as they walk they like to touch things, it is not enough just to see. The variety of sights, sounds, textures and scents speaks to them of the infinite care the Creator has taken with his creation.

These are practical, realistic people who like to

deal in clear facts rather than theories or abstract notions and ideas. They have need of something tangible to take them to the intangible. It is often hard for them to switch from the known and the seen to the unseen, imprecise world of the spiritual realm unless they can begin by using their senses. Some may like to look at a picture of nature, or one that is connected to some particular interest they have. Some just like to revel in colour, or to spend time contemplating an icon that will point them to God. A beautiful, fragrant flower that can be seen and touched and smelled, utilising three of the five senses, is likely to evoke wonder at the intricate detail of its parts, and can be the springboard to a time of prayer with God. Psalm 92 verses 4 and 5 seem to sum up this whole attitude in the words 'For you make me glad by your deeds, O LORD; I sing for joy at the work of your hands. How great are your works, O LORD, how profound your thoughts!'

Of course many people with quite different personality preferences find that from time to time their senses lead them to a spontaneous appreciation of, and conscious contact with, God. For instance, I have a very simple little stone figurine of a person kneeling, head bowed. Often I will reflect on that as I begin my prayer. If its back is towards me and on that day it seems as though my back is towards God for whatever reason then I may start by acknowledging that this is where I am in relation to him at this moment. On other days that figure has not changed at all but it seems to me to be expressing something quite different, and then that is where I might begin my prayer. My garden faces west and often in the summer there are spectacular sunsets. I look up from my weeding and an automatic, instinctive cry of wonder and of praise is literally wrung from my lips. For me these things are, as it were, a bonus, an extra; they are not something I actually depend on to draw me consciously towards God as do those who are more reliant on their senses.

Another gateway into prayer for sensing people, although not of course confined to them, is often music.

They may like simply to listen to it, or to join in and sing out their praises. They may like to sing impromptu, or by accompanying one of the many worship tapes available. Some find that praying aloud helps them because this engages both their senses and their whole bodies. And sometimes they want their bodies to help them express their prayer. They may hold their hands open, palms upward, to express that they are open to God and waiting to receive from him. Sometimes they may feel the need to kneel in penitence, or to actually prostrate themselves in awe before him. The simple gesture of holding up the hands in praise can help to express adoration, especially at those times when circumstances or emotions are making it hard to get going. A few people I know even like to dance out their joy or sorrow or whatever they wish to express and explore.

The place of prayer can be every bit as important as the posture adopted during prayer for those whose senses inform and shape their lives. Some have their favourite places out of doors; wide open windswept moors, leafy woodland walks, or anywhere where there is a large expanse of sky, and in urban areas, a particular route through the park or around quiet back streets. Those who prefer to pray indoors often make a special place for themselves. If it cannot be a permanent or a regular place then they may find it helpful to have well-chosen objects that they can set before them wherever they settle to pray each day. The objects might be chosen for their colour, or shape, or texture or for the memories that they hold and the associations that they evoke. Visual symbols like candles, a cross or an icon, help to hold the gaze and direct the attention. If kneeling is important then having an attractive prayer-stool or special cushion on which to do so will be a further aid to prayer.

Often they find it helpful to read prayers that others have written. Sometimes the act of copying out a prayer from a book and perhaps pasting in a suitable photograph or other illustration, then praying the prayer out loud is especially meaningful for them. Using prayers composed by others more skilled with words can at times release a new fount of prayer in them when their own has dried up. It is also a way of deliberately participating in the communion of saints. Familiarity with the words can be very important, and the prayer of repetition is often meaningful. As one friend put it, 'When you know the words off by heart then you can concentrate on the meaning instead of trying to figure out what you want to say.' And repetition is frequently an aid to contemplation.

Recently there has been a revival of interest in Celtic spirituality. They seem to have had a prayer for every activity. There are ones for waking up, getting dressed, lighting the fire, digging the soil, going on a journey and retiring at night. David Adam has published several collections of prayers in this tradition. In *Power Lines, Celtic Prayers About Work*,[1] he has included a section on the city. There are prayers based on the commuter rush hour, an escalator, a furnace and a crane, amongst others. Anything can be the start of prayer for those who are oriented towards God.

Just as sensing people like order and predictability in their everyday lives so many of them find it helpful to have a set order to their prayers, in private as well as in public. They may follow an acronym like ACTS, reminding them to include in due order the aspects of adoration, confession, thanksgiving and supplication. Others like to slowly pray through the Lord's Prayer phrase by phrase, amplifying the content of each as they go. Such ways may be the regular pattern for some, while for others they are more often a help to fall back on at times when they do not actually *feel* like praying. They utilise their wills to pray and follow a proven pattern despite their lack of ardour at the time.

To assist them in their intercessions these are people who may like to keep a detailed prayer list, or diary. Many find it helpful to use the monthly or quarterly sheets of prayer requests and news put out by various organisations and societies. Because they like to do things properly, exactly as instructed or requested, there is a danger that they may allow themselves to become overwhelmed by the sheer number of requests to pray for people and situations. When this is so they need to remind themselves of the principle behind pruning, and learn to cull the number of such lists they receive and retain. If they wish to receive the magazine but are not making use of the prayer requests on any regular basis then it will take great discipline to bin those unwanted lists immediately – the alternative is most probably for them to go on feeling unnecessarily guilty as all those bits of paper sit around unused.

Generally their style of prayer, like their usual mode of conversation, is simple in content and direct in expression. What is, simply is, without any need of amplification or explanation. They have a way of expressing profound things in a plain, open and immediate way, without any ambiguity. Their initial contact with God also needs to be in the actual here and now. For them, more than for those of any other personality structure, 'now is the accepted time . . . now is the day of salvation' (2 Cor 6:2 AV). They have a real need to know and feel that God is with them *today*, for they have no other time scale. As one troubled person put it 'If God is not with me now, it's as though he does not exist'. That man was genuinely unable to spontaneously recall any of the undoubted times in the past when the presence of God had been real for him. He needed to be gently reminded of them and of their relevance to his current situation. He needed help to re-establish communion with God in very tangible ways.

For sensing people, their initial contact with God is to find him embodied in nature and all his creation, and through the tangible elements of the sacraments. They tend to concentrate wholeheartedly on the present moment and on present experiences. Like the sheepdogs described earlier, every part of them is fully focussed on what they are doing. They are alert to every communication from God in whatever perceptible way he reveals himself. Being people of the senses they are very aware of their bodies, and of the material world around them. They can readily identify with the God who is closer to them even than these things, provided they can begin to contact him through them. They respond to God who is indeed incarnate. Sometimes they are so aware of his presence that, like good friends at ease in each other's company, words are unnecessary. They may even be an intrusion. There are times when words are unable to convey the wonder, delight, sorrow or confusion being experienced.

At those times, just to be in the company of a sympathetic, supportive Other is all that is required. This has been called the prayer of simple presence, or of simple regard. Simple does not mean simplistic, it means being as a little child, content to just be. Jesus taught that 'anyone who will not receive the kingdom of God like a little child will never enter it' (Mark 10:15). All of us, whatever our personality structure, need to cultivate this attitude of being fully aware of the present moment. Those for whom this does not come naturally can learn from those people of the senses for whom it does.

People who extravert their senses tend to be active in prayer, as in everything else. Often they like to converse with God aloud about whatever is concerning them at that moment. When words seem insufficient or too elusive they may like to express their deepest longings in some more tangible and expressive way. Making marks on different surfaces, whether or not the drawing or painting is meaningful to anyone else, is a useful vehicle for some. Others prefer model making, sculpture, singing or dancing. Yet others prefer to express their devotion in more immediately practical ways, as in their concern for and care of the church fabric, or its financial affairs.

Order, predictability and routine are generally important for many of those who like focussed prayer. They want to establish a pattern regarding regular times of prayer, the use of Scripture and other spiritual reading, and attendance at church. Whether or not they set it out in writing, they are likely to have definite goals in such matters, and to have evolved a rule of life to which they expect themselves to adhere. They are most comfortable and most free when they have defined, sometimes in considerable detail, what their aims are. If they have fixed with themselves to read for ten minutes and pray for fifteen before coffee each morning, or on the train to or from work, or at another set time, then all element of doubt is removed and they are free to do other things around these important ones.

There is a danger that this attitude of wanting to 'do things the right way' and 'keep the rules', might get out of control and begin to take over the person's life. Instead of serving him it becomes a hindrance and a dead weight. What began as a means to freedom can get out of proportion and lead to rigidity instead of fostering growth. I remember a nurse who caused consternation many years ago because one day she overslept and felt that she could not go straight on duty until she had had her 'quiet time'. Clearly that was being far too inflexible. The fact that others were having to wait to get off duty seemed to escape her.

Sometimes people find themselves praying in ways that are out of character with their personality as described so far. This can be very disconcerting for them, but in all probability they will be using a style that would be very familiar to the people we will look at in the next chapter. What seems to happen is that once having established themselves in their own way of praying they move on – or are moved on by the

Holy Spirit. Someone has suggested that because we have so much less conscious control over the latent aspects of our personalities, God is able to use those very characteristics to get through to us more clearly. For instance, someone who is normally precise and well planned in their approach to prayer may one day find that they are unaccountably 'waffling' instead.

What is happening is that they have probably switched into praying in the butterfly or beach-combing manner that is more characteristic of intuitive people. Their natural tendency then is to consider that these tantalising and fleeting thoughts must be distractions, and so of course they want to resist them. It is perhaps a new idea for them to allow themselves to just go with the flow – having first asked God to show them if they are in danger of drifting out of contact with him. Until he shows them otherwise they might try and welcome this new way of praying. They might even manage to allow themselves to float in an unfocussed way, going where he chooses to take them. Prayer in this way is a time of just musing with God, trusting him to bring to their attention whatever he wishes. It is not mooning if the focus of the musing is on God.

Main Features of Focussed Prayer

- Only one time span – the immediate present.
- Uses tangible, sensory symbols as pointers to the intangible and the unseen. Candles, pictures, icons, banners, fragrant flowers, a cross, music can all be helpful.
- Bodily posture is an important part of this prayer.

- Predictability is significant; prayer lists may be helpful.

Points to Ponder

- Pruning lists when they get unwieldy makes for stronger growth.
- Rites and rituals helpful to oneself must not be. unwittingly imposed on others.

Pitfalls to Avoid

- Getting bogged down in ritual and right order so that spontaneity is lost.
- A rule of life can turn into rigidity.

Prayer Exercises

1. Read Matthew chapter 6, verses 25–34.

   - Thank God for the sharpness of your senses.
   - Praise him for the variety and diversity of all living things, and in the elements, the sky, the wind and the weather, the sun and the stars.
   - Ask his forgiveness for any times you have misused your senses, either allowing them to take too prominent a place in your life, or neglecting them.
   - Bring your worries to him, the small as well as the great ones.

- Now re-read verse 33 and turn it into your own prayer.
- If it seems helpful, write down the result of your reflection.

2. Take a psalm, or a portion of one; read it meditatively; apply it to your own situation. As you do this regularly make a note for future reference of which psalms to read when sad, confused, rejoicing, angry, anxious or whatever you find there.

3. Go for a prayer walk.

   Deliberately use each of your five senses one by one. Turn what you see, and hear, and touch, and smell into a prayer of praise, wonder, intercession and petition.

   Then let your thoughts wander where they will. Be a butterfly, flitting from topic to topic at random.

   Find an object, a fallen leaf, a stone, a feather, even a discarded wrapper, and take it home to remind you to go on praying about whatever was most preoccupying you on this walk.

3

Musing With God

A considerable number of people are inclined to
view the world with the eye of the imagination
rather than with that of their physical body. They
are people who enjoy speculating on what might
be rather than dwelling on what actually is. The
price they pay for this is that they usually develop
their imagination somewhat at the expense of being
observant. They are generally quick to grasp the big
picture and they like to take the wide approach. They
can see the potential of a scheme but are likely to
be impatient if required to trace it through in any
detail. Usually they have little interest in facts and
figures or specifics of any sort. For them theories
and hunches are more real than individual items.
It is possibilities that matter because for them
these are the 'facts of the future', and it is future
possibility rather than present reality which holds
their interest.

These people are good at seeing the overall pattern
and the global scheme of things but may not know
how they arrived at such a panoramic view. They
have picked up vibes and impressions, and seem able
to read the situation without knowing quite how they
have done so. These are the forward-looking people
who are often so interested in what is on, or just
beyond, the horizon that they sometimes miss what

is happening around them at this moment. It seems as though for them, what is going on today is not really interesting in its own right. They use it just as a stepping-stone for tomorrow. I've heard it said that they tend to be so much into the future that they are 'not quite all here'.

Such people often function best and achieve most when they are able to do things on the spur of the moment. They are seldom comfortable or productive when having to work to a prearranged schedule. They can work all day and all night if something interests them and they are inspired to do it. When they have no interest in the job they quickly become exhausted after doing relatively little. They dislike having to follow instructions and they seldom work in an orderly, predictable way. It would seldom occur to them to begin with step one and then proceed through each succeeding step in turn, without missing any out. Their pattern is to 'guess how', using their intuitive grasp of what needs to be done. They are liable to begin part way through a sequence and to miss out some stages, yet despite this they generally manage to get most things done satisfactorily. They tend to dislike repetition and sameness. As a consequence they are likely to become bored and quickly lose interest when there are no enticing possibilities around, and no changes taking place.

In conversation they tend to be complex as they seldom take things at face value. They see so many possibilities in what you say that they just cannot give you a concise statement or answer in reply. They will skirmish all around the subject, and this tendency is aptly summed up in the saying 'Ask them the time and they will tell you how a clock works'. They see lots of connections and are prone to leap to conclusions on minimal factual evidence, having made associations that astound and amaze others. Their tendency is to employ generalised concepts with a liberal use of metaphor and analogy. They seldom give hard facts so that others can assess their proposals. They are apt to present their ideas and insights using the broad brush approach, telling their dream but giving absolutely no detail for others to grasp hold of.

Such are the intuitive people, and I am using that word in its technical rather than its common usage. Popular myth has it that intuition is a female characteristic, most likely to find expression in poetry or prophecy, but this is not my meaning at all. For a start there is no gender bias in its distribution. I am using the words intuitive and intuition to denote people who get their information by hunches, in an immediate and almost complete way, rather like a speeded-up video film. They do not see any details at all but they do know the end result, their conclusion, speedily and accurately. It is a way of perceiving, of finding out about the world we live in, that is quite different from that of using the five bodily senses. Not surprisingly it results in quite a different way of praying.

Jesus showed his intuitive side whenever he spoke in parables, and when he employed similes. He often used the phrase 'it is like . . .', making intuitive connections and deductions that his hearers may not have grasped for themselves.

As we might expect, intuitive people tend to pray as they talk; often wandering all round the subject, taking detours as each new concept or idea or question occurs to them. They make many connections between things and events that would seem quite disparate to people of other personalities. They have a tendency to see possibilities that just do not occur to other people. They can quickly see signs and symbols where others do not perceive them, and seem able to find at least one alternative meaning for almost everything. Because they pass quickly from one item to another as it occurs to them their prayer is rather like the feeding foray of a butterfly, never seeming to settle anywhere for long. They appear to flit from one topic to another without any apparent connectedness that other people can grasp. Like a butterfly they alight only momentarily on any one flower, on any one topic, and then they are off again flitting about with no very evident destination.

The prayer of intuitive people often utilises few words. They are engaged in a mystery beyond language, and by their very nature are happy in such an environment. In his book *Pray Your Way*, Bruce Duncan has described this style of prayer as

like wandering along the beach, waiting to see what the sea washes up. Much of it is useless flotsam and jetsam. Ideas float around, images come and go, and now and again in this loose and relaxed freewheeling way of communing with God (and this prayer must always be 'with God', not ego-centred daydreaming) significant perceptions occur . . . People come to mind. Things to be done come to mind. It is prayer of intuitive association guided by the Holy Spirit.[1]

The prayer of those who extravert their intuition is of course somewhat different from that of those who use the same function in the introverted way. To quote from Bruce Duncan again

Extraverted intuition scans the outer world like a minesweeper, picking up any perceptions that have special meaning. So extraverted . . . prayer is always seeking to find new and ingenious ways of co-operating with God to transform the world into God's Kingdom. The inner vision alone is not enough, unless it can be turned into external reality.[2]

By contrast the same author goes on to describe

contemplation . . . in which you are totally absorbed in a state of emptiness and almost non-being, out of touch with time and place, is essentially introverted. So also is the fantasy prayer in which we pay attention to God through freewheeling intuitive association. The Australian aboriginal 'Walkabout' is one image of introverted [intuitive] prayer, a long, solitary and contemplative journey into the mysterious interior wasteland.[3]

Intuitive people are always pressing on, either out into the world like a minesweeper, or inwards towards the mysterious hinterland as if they are on a solo aboriginal walkabout. It is characteristic of them that they always want more. They are in fact the most audacious Oliver Twists of the spiritual life, and therein lies a danger, though it is more for *other* people than for themselves. Because they have such a wide-ranging curiosity themselves they can easily fall into the trap of assuming that everyone else has a similarly extensive spiritual appetite. It is sometimes difficult for them to realise that people of other personalities do not want or need to go as far out into the great ocean of God as they themselves desire and delight to do.

One of the pitfalls for them is that they may attempt to entice other people too far (too far for the other, that is) out to sea so that they become out of their depth. They really do need to remember that some people are liable to take fright, and if they do so they may never venture to get even their feet wet again. They have to remind themselves that the spirituality of those with other personality characteristics is often quite different. It may be of a kind that does better nearer the known shores, or making their own discoveries in the confines of rock pools, rather than out in the fathomless depths.

A combination of their particular personality traits often leads intuitive people into doing things so thoroughly in their imagination that they sometimes omit to actually carry them out in reality. It may be while they are enjoying a shower, or when they are out digging the garden, that they are suddenly able to put together an excellent reply to a difficult letter. After waiting in vain many days for the expected response it might finally dawn on the intuitive person that perhaps he only dreamed up that brilliant answer. Maybe he never actually wrote the letter, and if he did write it perhaps he did not get around to sending it off. There are just too many stages between the dream of an intuitive person and the completion of any necessary action. Similarly it is often difficult for intuitive people to know whether they have spent their prayer time in their own dreamy imagination, or whether they have really been in communion with God.

44

Intuitive people tend to value silence for much of their prayer, since there is just so much going on for them, in their wordless butterfly way. In this those who extravert their intuitive function are different from most other extraverts. They appreciate and need far more quiet than any other extravert does. There is a danger that they might generalise this particular requirement of theirs and assume that all other people have a need for as much silence and stillness as they like to have. The fact is that many others have a lesser need of silence when they pray in their own particular way and they are more comfortable with rather less of it than the intuitive person finds essential.

A quotation which I heard some years ago, and now regret that I did not obtain the source of at the time, goes 'The liturgy is a God-flavoured noise before we get down to the quiet, the real prayer'. If that sentence had only been prefaced with the three words 'for some people . . .' (or, if using this framework, 'for an intuitive . . .') it would then be more accurate. Such a proviso would also help to prevent much unnecessary guilt in those people who just do not have the same capacity for, or derive as much benefit from, silence as the writer of that telling sentence evidently obtains. As it stands that sentence appears to make the arrogant assumption that all other prayer is of lesser value and not 'real prayer' at all.

We all do well to remember that differences are not deficiencies.

Although it might seem churlish to take just one sentence from a book that really does help us to see silence in context, I find myself wanting to add a somewhat similar qualifying clause when I read what David Runcorn writes in his excellent book *Space for God.*

He says '. . . silence has a way of expressing presence more profoundly than words'.[4] If only he had prefaced that and similar statements with a proviso like 'for some people . . .' it might have helped many more to realise how precious silence can become when persisted with. As it stands it runs the risk of leaving a number of people feeling inadequate and less spiritual, if not actually unspiritual, because for them presence is manifested and expressed quite differently.

Intuitive people are generally eager to share with others the reflections and insights that have come to them in prayer. Sharing helps them to go on and discover yet further possibilities, and to gain fresh insights. All intuitives tend to like the opportunity to share with others in order to progress and grow in the spiritual life, although there is a difference in how they will be comfortable in doing so. Those who extravert their intuition are generally happy to share with anyone who will listen. Those who introvert their intuition are likely to be more comfortable sharing with a small number of people whom they both know and trust. They need to feel safe before they can venture to share that which is so precious to them.

We have seen that intuitive people are drawn more towards searching out the possibilities inherent in a situation, rather than to working with what is actual and present and factual. They are highly imaginative people and are seldom able to be satisfied for long, if at all, with things as they have always been. They are stimulated by change, by the potential that each alteration in the status quo presents. They thrive best when there is plenty of variety in their lives. Without change and variety they can easily get very bored, and this may affect their prayer life.

At times any change anywhere in their lives may be enough to bring new life and fresh enthusiasm into their prayer. At other times they may need to make some deliberate changes in their manner or pattern of private prayer if they are to overcome this tendency to sink into a debilitating boredom. And sometimes it may be necessary to consider a cause that has nothing at all to do with their personality make-up. Discernment is required. Does the lack of interest in and zest for prayer stem from a lack of the variety that is so necessary to keep intuitive people going? Or is it the result of the person resisting something that God is trying to bring to their attention? The remedy for the latter of course is to stick with the discomfort and the 'boredom' until they are able to find out what God is wanting to say to them.

To combat their prevailing tendency to boredom they need to augment their distinctively intuitive prayer style with something of the pattern that is outlined in one or other of the next two chapters. If they are drawn towards loving God with all their minds they will be helped by structuring their prayer within a well thought out theological framework. They can help themselves to combat boredom by developing a thorough understanding of the faith. If they are drawn more towards loving God with all their hearts they will want their prayer to be more of a wholistic response. It must involve all of their being, enabling them to experience their faith more than to understand it. They will combat boredom by occupying themselves in searching out the possibilities such faith offers for the development of people.

In the first of his *Letters to Malcolm*, C.S. Lewis uses the very descriptive phrase 'the Liturgical Fidget'.[5] I suspect this is a trap that extrovert intuitive people are peculiarly likely to fall into. If they are in a position to introduce or recommend change in public worship they have great responsibility. They must discern whether the change in question is really needed by the congregation, for whatever reason. Perhaps they are taking the opportunity to introduce change more to meet their own personal need for variety than for any objective congregational, liturgical or doctrinal necessity.

When their attention wanders, the spiritual interest of intuitive people may often be restored by something as simple as a change in reading matter. Moving from reading Scripture that is mainly historical or ceremonial in content to something that is predominantly symbolic, may fire their imagination into renewed enthusiasm for an encounter with God. Reading the parables of Jesus where he poses questions but does not provide the answers, parables which stand on their own without any explanation being given, may revive their flagging interest. They will respond to the challenge of working out a number of possible answers. Or they may find that they are able to draw inspiration from the richly symbolic chapters of books like Daniel, Ezekiel and Revelation.

Intuitive people have wide horizons. As they notice patterns and trends rather than specific detail and are easily drawn into symbolism, much of their prayer will therefore be derived from reflections and insights gleaned during their daily activities.

48

Books and articles read, conversations held, news bulletins they have heard and TV documentaries seen; all information and awareness that has captured their imagination becomes incorporated into their wordless, beachcombing prayer,

In order to supplement this naturally free-ranging prayer style, intuitive people may find it helpful at times to deliberately pray in a manner more reminiscent of that described in the last chapter. They can help themselves to do this by making a conscious effort to slow down. They often need to slow down physically and outwardly in order to be able to slow down their inner pace also. When they are able to do this it will help them to bring the focus of their attention back from somewhere over the horizon and into the present moment.

One way of concentrating on actual events in the here and now is to make the effort to consciously use each of your senses in turn. Try using those odd moments during the day when you are waiting for something – for the bus, for a meeting to get going, for the oven timer to ping, or for someone to come to the phone. Use those moments to tune in to the reality of the here and now world to which you may be a relative stranger. What can you hear – traffic noises, children playing, machinery working somewhere, birds singing or perhaps a distant aeroplane. Notice what you hear, pay attention to it and turn it into a prayer for the people generating the sounds, or into thanksgiving for your ability to hear so well.

Notice too the aromas that surround you; the scent of fresh flowers or coffee, or the dusty street or vehicle exhaust. Consciously notice each of the scents that you catch and let your sense of smell lead you into an awareness of the present moment. Then concentrate on being aware of the different textures that surround you. Pay attention to the texture of your own clothing, to the roughness of the wall beside you and the smoothness of the pole for the bus stop sign. Wake up your feet and become aware of the surface you are standing on, and notice the feel of the breeze as it ruffles your hair or brushes your face.

Sharpen your powers of observation by playing games with yourself. Count how many different types of chimney pot, front door or window you can discover as you look around you with your newly-awakened and concentrated attention. See if you can taste anything in the air, salt from the sea perhaps.

In the longer term sharpen your ability to really hear by consciously listening to music. Pay attention to the detail and try to pick out the various components. Enjoy the music for its tempo and its beat, its rhythm and its resonance in this present moment, rather than for something it leads you into speculating about. Use your eyes and your mind to really look at pictures; see each element as well as the general composition, tone and mood it conveys. Notice where there is fine detail and where there is not so that you really read the picture instead of glancing over it on your way to something else.

Take this heightened power of observation into your prayer. Pick, or buy, a flower; gaze on this natural work of art and let it lead you to the Creator. Feel the differing textures of the stalk and of the leaves as well as the parts of the flower itself. Savour the scent, however elusive it may be. Another day you might like to light a candle instead, and watch the different shapes the flame makes, and the way it bends with every breath of air. Let this speak to you of the Holy Spirit, and recall his ministry to us in prayer. Often we do not know how to pray about a situation 'but the Spirit himself intercedes for us with groans that words cannot express' (Rom 8:26). In good weather go for a walk in the country, or in a park, along a canal, river bank or quiet street. Deliberately use all your senses in turn, praising God for the many sounds and sights, the scents and textures that his infinite creativity has placed all around you.

It is also important to become aware of your body as you pray. Your natural tendency is probably to let your imagination give you a sense of yourself kneeling or prostrate or dancing or turning away from the Lord, without you ever moving a muscle. Your imagined actions are that real to you. Sometimes use your body to actually do such things, allow yourself to try kneeling while you are at prayer, or to raise your hands and your voice as you pray. Even experiment with actually dancing out your prayer before the Lord, instead of being content to imagine yourself doing so.

God has made us as bodily people, not as disembodied pure spirits. There are times when it is helpful to allow our bodies to lead us into prayer. As a way of finding God in the present moment train yourself to be aware of changes that take place in your body. If some muscle groups are particularly tense, note this, and reflect on possible reasons for the tension. In this way you will be letting your body lead you into prayer for the situations and people that are causing you to be tense. Be aware of changes in your mood too. Let joy as well as sorrow, excitement as well as pain, lead you to the presence of God who loves you and cares for you.

Watch little children in their total absorption in what they are doing at any given moment, and take such an attitude into your prayer. And instead of praying anywhere and in any posture, experiment with making a special prayer place in some area of the house. Take care in selecting the objects you will have there; a vase of flowers or an ornament, a stone or a shell that is particularly meaningful for you or that you just find attractive. Choose the colours that you want to have about you as you pray. Select a stool or a cushion to kneel or sit on, and a cross or candle or icon to hold your gaze. This is all part of being aware of the actual and the here and now as you enter more fully into a relationship with God. He is both transcendent and immanent, both knowable and approachable and yet the One who can never be fully known.

Main Features of 'Musing' Prayer

- It is unfocussed, diffuse and wide ranging, like a butterfly or a beachcomber.
- It is sustained by variety and change.
- It thrives on silence, even for the extraverts as they scan the world like a minesweeper.
- It is enriched by sharing, even for the introverts after they have been on their internal walkabout.

Points to Ponder

- Boredom can be a problem. Discern whether it stems from lack of variety elsewhere in your life, or from a too unchanging pattern of prayer, or from resisting God in some area.

- Try switching to reading Scripture that is more symbolic than factual, like Daniel, Ezekiel, John and Revelation, or to the parables that pose questions but do not give any answers.

Pitfalls to Avoid

- Making the assumption that everyone else requires as much silence as you do.
- The temptation to encourage other people to go out of their depth just because you like to do so.

Prayer Exercises

1. Recollect that you are in the presence of God, then wander along the beach of your whole being with him, prayerfully waiting to discover what the sea of your consciousness washes up.

2. Imagine yourself to be a butterfly. Go with God wherever your thoughts and feelings take you. Draw into your prayer all your experiences and all your disconnected thoughts. Bring into the immediate presence of God everything that vies for your attention.

3. Allow yourself to float in the ocean of the love of God. Know that you are kept afloat by the density of that never failing love. Feel yourself being upheld by his constant presence within you. Pay careful attention to anything that he

brings to your notice, asking him to show you what he wishes you to do about it.

4. Read Numbers chapter 13 verses 26–33.

   • Reflect on the different characters, and their motivation.
   • Who did you side with? The majority who saw the practical difficulties, the two who saw possibilities in the situation, or Moses who had to hear what God wanted?
   • What principles emerge in this chapter and the next?

5. To encourage yourself to be more focussed, occasionally try one of the exercises at the end of the previous chapter.

Loving God with the Mind

Now we turn our attention to those people who like to direct their lives mainly through their intellect. They have very different values and desires from those who tend to run their lives according to what they are learning from their senses, the people we considered in chapter two. They also differ quite markedly from those we looked at in the last chapter, who tend to rely largely on their intuitive insights without knowing exactly how they formed their opinions. The people we are looking at now usually like to be exact, and because of this they can sometimes seem to be exacting to and of others. They take nothing for granted, and are always seeking answers to questions about life in general and about the meaning of Life in particular.

The group of people we are now considering seem to run their lives almost as if their motto were 'to live is to UNDERSTAND'. They simply must understand the world and the universe that they live in. They have enquiring minds. From an early age they are likely to have bombarded those around them with persistent questions about the meaning of things. They are constantly asking 'why?' They cannot be fobbed off with an ill-thought-out or incomprehensible reply. Any answer that does not satisfy their intellectual curiosity is likely to be treated with considerable disdain. Alternative sources of information and enlightenment will be somewhat relentlessly pursued until their thirst for truth is satisfied. It is absolutely imperative for them that their world makes logical, consistent and reliable sense.

They love to analyse and to conceptualise, and to seek out the overall principle underlying anything that is engaging their attention. They seem to have the ability to remain objective and detached, and so they are able to examine things and situations in a dispassionate way. This attitude can sometimes be quite unnerving to those who do not have the same ability. It is particularly likely to be incomprehensible to those who love God primarily with their hearts, the ones we will be considering in the next chapter. The ones we are looking at now are likely to make their decisions on the basis of whether, having weighed up all sides of the matter, one decision seems to be right, and for that reason all others will be wrong. Often this attitude seems incredibly black and white to those who do not share it. Such a reliance on principle can seem to overrule or cut out proper consideration of how application of that principle might affect the people it will inevitably bear upon. And issues concerning people are seldom completely clearcut.

Another aspect of this detachment is the ability to do a good job even when doing that particular job cuts across some personal option. If the principles are right and the job needs to be done, and it clearly falls within this person's sphere of responsibility, then his own wishes simply have no place in the decision. Such people have the ability to recognise personal considerations and then to lay them on one side, regarding them as utterly irrelevant to getting the task done. These are goal-oriented people who concentrate on objectives and on getting specific tasks done. In doing so they are sometimes in danger of overlooking the people who will be engaged in carrying out those tasks and duties.

Not surprisingly this group are called Analysts, or Thinkers. In calling them this there is no implication that others do not also analyse or think things through logically. Of course many others do when it is necessary but such processes are not their mainspring, their chief characteristics, as they are for those we are considering in this chapter.

Jesus demonstrated his use of the 'thinking' attitude in his teaching whenever he drew attention to an underlying principle. It is also apparent in the story of a rich young man who asked Jesus what he must do to gain eternal life. He received a résumé of the commandments, and in response he said that he had always kept them. 'Jesus looked at him and loved him', and then went on to outline the bottom line. 'Go, sell everything you have and give to the poor, and you will have treasure in heaven. Then come, follow me' (Mark 10:17–21). This requirement proved too hard for the young man. His face fell, and he went away sad. It takes considerable detachment to let someone go away at that point, and in that state, a detachment that is a particularly 'thinking' trait.

Another of their characteristics is that they tend to have very high standards, which they apply first to themselves, but do not stop there. They also expect everyone else to be using the same criteria. They have a natural tendency to find and point out the flaws in anything that has been done or is proposed.

Their motive for this is that when they point out any minor blemishes that they detect, these can then be rectified. When that is done then something which is already good as it stands will become really excellent. This tendency to give a critique whenever their opinion is sought is quite likely to be received by people with different personalities as criticism, and when this happens the potentially useful critique element is lost. It is just not heard because the feelings of the recipient have been unwittingly so hurt. Even if thinkers do pick up the hurt feelings of others this would not deter them from their habit of offering a critique. They are motivated by the pursuit of truth and excellence rather than by a quest for harmony.

The likelihood of friction between these people and those with a different personality make-up is further increased by their tendency to state their position bluntly. They do not go in for padding, or for wrapping something up gently so that it becomes more acceptable. They are very much of the 'call a spade a spade' brigade. Even if they are at all aware of their own feelings, they will expect their objective logic to overide their subjective emotions. Since they are able to discount their own feelings they can all too easily overlook how important the emotional side of things is for others. All of these factors combine to ensure that the prayer which comes most naturally to them is likely to be different from all the other types we are considering.

Thinkers require exactly the same principles to govern their prayer as those that guide and determine everything else to which they set their hands and their minds. They like to engage in an orderly progression of thought, proceeding logically from cause through to its effect, considering things from their beginning through to a conclusion. For them the key elements of prayer are their search for Truth and Justice, and they respond most readily to those aspects of God which notably reveal these traits. They tend to see God most clearly as Logos, the Word of God who is eternal Truth; as King, Divine Lawgiver, and as Judge of all.

First and foremost they must be able to understand God through their minds. The study of Scripture and of theology is very much an integral part of their prayer.

For people with a different personality make-up such study is often more of a preliminary activity, a leading into prayer rather than constituting the prayer itself. Whatever concept or idea or truth they are pursuing, thinkers like to study a subject from every possible angle. In particular they like to know the principles on which it is based. It is as though they take a mental walk all around their subject, and scrutinise it from all sides before they are satisfied that they really do understand it. They have a great need and a real desire to understand their faith and generally speaking they are not particularly concerned about also being able to experience it. Their need and their overwhelming aspiration is to understand so that they will be able to predict and to explain reality.

In order to take the totality of their understanding further, the prayer of these people often contains a lot of questions. At times it may even take on an argumentative quality as they wrestle with God about the principles that govern the universe. This is not a search for intellectual knowledge alone. They have a genuine desire that the knowledge gained should lead on to any necessary change in their belief and in their behaviour. They have a real desire to get at the truth of any matter in order that the truth may set them free.

Since for them the essence of prayer is to open their minds to the mind of the Infinite, the high point of prayer for thinkers is likely to be the moment of intellectual insight. They relate to God just as they relate to other people, in a willed, unemotional, disciplined and dispassionate way. It is then a logical step for them to move on from any new insight about God, his laws and his universe, to considering the implications in their own life, and of course to make any necessary changes.

They desire to be objective in prayer as much as in the rest of their lives, and they like to objectify their spirituality in order to be able to explain it. They reason that if they cannot explain something then they have not understood it, and understand they must. Their prayer is very much that of loving God with all their mind, and it was probably this approach that Thomas Aquinas was writing about when he used the phrase 'a rational gazing on God'.

In their pursuit of truth these people can be very self-critical. They often have an almost ruthlessly objective honesty in appraising their own behaviour and attitude. Their ability to confront when necessary means that they are also willing to face up to unpalatable truths about themselves when these become apparent to them.

Because of their intellectual, rational and objective style of argumentative prayer, wrestling with God over great issues, some thinkers may never have had a peak personal experience of God. As a result they may sometimes, in some company, feel inadequate, as though they may be missing out on something vital. They do well to remind themselves that God can be apprehended as well through the mind as through the emotions. Their own particular relationship with God, though different, is every bit as valid as some more colourful ones that seem to make the news these days. They have a tendency to be impatient with repetition in devotional expression, and they generally dislike the trend for singing choruses, often several times, rather than doctrinal hymns in public worship. Sometimes it is a real battle for them not to despise emotion. They have a tendency to confuse it with emotionalism and to dismiss emotion altogether.

Thinkers who are also extraverts are likely to go out from prayer and get involved in social and political issues, challenging current ideas and fads. Sometimes prophetic action out in the world may actually be their prayer itself, as it was for Hosea. For those who introvert their thinking function, prayer is more likely to be a private and an individual matter, an inner wrestling with God as Jacob wrestled alone until daybreak. Sometimes their wrestling may be over some issue raised in TV documentaries or newspaper articles, in order to understand the application of doctrine to the matter. If they are then constrained to take any action this is likely to take the form of writing a well-reasoned letter to the appropriate authority, or to the media. People with different personalities might be more prone to going on a protest march or lobbying their MP in person.

When well settled in their own style of prayer thinkers can be greatly enriched if, from time to time, they extend their prayer repertoire. As with all the other personalities that we have considered, it is helpful to include elements that initially come more naturally to the others. Some find that emotions and the whole feeling side of themselves can seem irrelevant in their pursuit of knowledge and intellectual understanding. Then when their feelings do begin to wake up, for any reason, and to impinge on their ordered existence this can be very bewildering and frightening for them.

One reason for irrational fears might be that other images are lurking alongside their conscious and biblically-based concepts of God as a welcome King and impartial Judge. Many individuals continue to have a number of barely conscious, and therefore hugely powerful, images of what C.S. Lewis called 'false half gods'.[1]

These false half gods can come in various guises. One of the most common is that of the Policeman god. He is always out to catch you even if you have only been scrumping apples from the garden of a derelict house. Others are dismayed by a strangely persistent Headmaster god, a most discouraging and disapproving personage. He is always telling them they could have done better and leaving them with the impression that they are somehow not up to the mark. Another variant of this is the stern, unsmiling Lord High Executioner. He listens to everybody else but not to me, and so I haven't a hope in his presence. And then there is the Pharaoh god, the slave driver. He insists on more and more work to a higher and higher standard with less material being provided and ever harsher penalties threatened if not enough is accomplished. No wonder the associated feelings of unease and impending retribution are so uncomfortable and so utterly incomprehensible to a rational mind!

Of course when we get around to recognising and naming these distorted half gods it is not difficult to see how they have arisen. They are formed out of a mixture of the particular personality traits of a still-immature young person, moulded by some of his more unfortunate childhood experiences. C.S. Lewis has pointed out that it is only when the false half gods go that the real God can come.

A good way to deal with half gods and other distortions is to acknowledge them, even though you are unlikely to welcome them. Acknowledge those uncomfortable, irrational feelings when they arise, and bring them into the prayer relationship with God. The natural tendency of thinkers is to dismiss those feelings of which they are aware. They can seem such a hindrance to what they regard as 'true prayer', centred on the mind and the intellect.

One way of encouraging an appropriate and acceptable emotional component to accompany the prayer of the mind is to engage in thanksgiving and praise. Begin with the mental concepts and then deliberately seek after a relevant emotion to go alongside the ideas. At first entering into the whole feeling realm may have to be thought through, in just the same way as everything else has to be approached through the mind. Recognition of emotions can be encouraged by the person asking himself 'What am I thankful for?' and then going on to also say to himself 'Given that I am thankful for these things, what feelings might be appropriate in these circumstances?'

Another way of beginning to get in touch with thankfulness is to practise thanking those people you come into contact with in the course of everyday life. Often thinkers seem to take people and the services they provide for granted. One man said in astonishment 'Of course I don't thank people for doing their job, only when they go beyond it'. They may well find it helpful to practise saying 'Thank you' to family members (especially spouse), their secretary or the person on the supermarket checkout. Also it will help them and others if they try and make a real point of affirming someone every single day.

One minute in such deliberate recollection and thanksgiving at the end of each day can soon get a person into the habit of not only being but also of feeling thankful. When he is comfortable with this approach it can then be extended, both in time and in content. If you want to supplement the habit of regular thanksgiving with a slightly more comprehensive incursion into the emotional realm, try asking yourself some questions designed to elicit your feelings. Ask yourself 'In what way might some feelings have been aroused today? When, and by what, were they awakened? When, and about what was I sad, angry, pleased, jealous or whatever else I began to be aware of, however remotely?'

Some people find to their astonishment that they have only a small vocabulary pertaining to the emotions. For them the first step may have to be to sit down with a dictionary and find as many words as they can for the various shades of different feelings. Others may prefer to find a friend with whom they can talk through the range of words that convey emotions, someone who is himself quite at home in the feeling area of life. Another useful ploy is to occasionally watch a TV soap with the sound turned off, and try to name the emotions that the characters display by their gestures, their expressions and their body language.

Reading is another way of becoming more familiar with emotions. As well as reading for knowledge try to be aware of any feelings that might accompany your thoughts. Read a poem once a week, and a novel at least once a year. In particular read the psalms regularly. Ask yourself what feelings are being written about and conveyed in each psalm. Then ask yourself if you have ever felt a similar emotion at any time. Have you yourself ever felt a similar anger, or joy, or sorrow or whatever feeling you detect? Train yourself to recognise the emotional component of your response as well as the intellectual element as you read, and then let that become part of your prayer.

In addition to becoming aware of your emotions you might ocasionally even dare to express them. This becomes slightly less daunting the more you manage to do it. Whenever you come to prayer try to be aware of the emotional aspect of your life over the previous twenty-four hours. Begin to bring your feelings as well as your thoughts and your questions into your prayer. If this seems strange, remember that you are bringing emotions to the very One who created them. They will not seem strange to him.

Main Features of 'Mind' Prayer

- Understanding an issue is crucial. Questions are often a prominent feature.
- There is an argumentative quality of wrestling with God over key issues.
- There is a great desire for intellectual honesty and integrity.

- The study of Scripture and of theology, and the application of doctrine, are important elements.
- A greater emphasis on loving God with all the mind, than of experiencing him with the heart.
- God is most readily worshipped as Logos, Word made flesh, Truth, King, Judge.

Points to Ponder

- What lingering false half gods prevent me from relating more fully to the true God? Name them. Draw them. Expose them.
- To be fully rounded prayer needs to involve the heart as well as the head. Dare to express your emotions in prayer.

Pitfalls to Avoid

- Despising emotion.
- Confusing a proper expression of emotion with sheer emotionalism.
- Feeling inadequate because your relationship with God may be different from the experiences reported by others.

Prayer Exercise

1. Read Luke chapter 18 verses 9–14.

    - As you read consider the following questions:
      - Why did Jesus tell this parable?
      - Who was he telling it for?

- What are the guiding principles behind this parable?
- When am I most self-satisfied?
- How do I look down on people?
- Who might I tend to look down on?

• Put names from your own family, friends and acquaintances into the sentence 'God, I thank you that I am not like . . ., or even like . . .'

• Ask yourself:
  - Where and when do I share the attitude of the Pharisee?
  - Have I ever prayed a prayer like that of the tax collector?
  - Is there anything I need to alter in my life as a result of reading this parable?
  - Is there anyone I need to forgive, or anyone to whom I need to make restitution?

• Dialogue with God about your understanding of this parable; listen for any changes he wants you to make in your life. Ask God to show you what small, achievable and repeatable steps you can take towards making this change. Then decide when you will implement the first step.

2. When you are ready to begin to develop more of a heart response to supplement that of your intellect, take the same passage on another occasion. This time see yourself as though you are in your own church but not as yourself; instead take some time to become each of the characters in turn.

- Are you standing, . . . sitting, . . . kneeling, . . . lounging?

— Where are you; in the front for all to see; in a dark corner near the back; or where?

— What are you feeling as the Pharisee, in that part of the church and in that particular posture?

— What are you feeling as the tax collector in your chosen part of the church and your particular posture?

— Where is Jesus; what is he doing and saying as your prayer proceeds?

• Let your imagination embellish the facts, and your heart respond to whatever emerges for you. Let your prayer arise from this awareness. Just let it unfold as it will.

5

Loving God with the Heart

We have seen that there is a wide variation in the way that people with different personalities relate to God. They differ in which aspect of God most appeals to them, and therefore to which they most readily and naturally respond. They also differ quite markedly in the actual way that they pray. There are a large number of people, men and women, for whom the most important aspect of prayer is to have a personal experience of God – a deeply-felt heart relationship with him. An experience *of* God is for them more important, and more precious, than any amount of knowledge *about* him. They desire to know God by what they experience of him, rather than because of anything they may understand about him with their heads.

The prayer that comes most naturally to them is likely to be people-centred. It is generally affective in nature, motivated and sustained (on the human level) by feelings and emotions. Indeed, many of the prayer features of those who love God with all their *minds*, the distinctive aspects of which we looked at in the last chapter, are probably regarded by these people as preparations for prayer. They do not seem to heart, or 'feeling', people to be actually prayer itself.

Certainly I remember listening with astonishment

to a friend talking about the 'loving God with all the mind' style of prayer. What she was calling prayer seemed to me to be more what I thought of as preparatory Bible study. I used the reading to lead me on to what I thought of as the 'real prayer'. We had quite a lively debate that taught me a great deal; it broadened my horizons and opened my understanding considerably.

That discussion was probably the start of my interest in the whole subject of how our natural personalities affect so profoundly our patterns of prayer. Previously I had unconsciously and rather arrogantly assumed, as indeed we all tend to do, that my way was 'the' way and others were possibly (dare I write it) aberrations.

For the people we are considering in this chapter, relationships are paramount. The quality of the relationships formed with the people they work with is generally of more importance than anything they manage to achieve by the work itself. Relationships are for them of more consequence than productivity or output. Also they tend to be more concerned about people than they are about abstract principles. They are generally more interested in the effect any decision may have on the people affected by it than they are in the principle on which the decision was based. They are likely to be somewhat more concerned with any mitigating circumstances there may be than they are about issues of absolute and impartial justice. That does not mean that they are disinterested in justice issues. It does mean that their concern for the people affected by such issues comes before a consideration of the principles behind any action that may be taken.

Jesus often acted and spoke on principle. He also

had a strong feeling side to his nature. He was always moved by suffering, and said the word or reached out a hand to heal, and he was conscious of the energy that this took (Mark 5:30). He was really joyful when the seventy-two disciples returned and showed that they had grasped something of his power and his mission (Luke 10:21). He was enraged when he found the traders had turned the Temple area into a market-place (Matt 21:12, 13). He was in anguish, deeply distressed and troubled, in the Garden of Gethsemane. There he showed his need for human company, as he had so often done at the home in Bethany (Mark 14:32–40; John 11:5). He was deeply moved and troubled by the death of Lazarus at which he wept publicly (John 11:33–35).

Feeling-oriented people are seldom as interested in abstract ideas, or in pure theology, as they are in the effect that ideas and theology have on the people who espouse them. The great doctrines of the faith tend to seem somewhat dry and uninteresting unless they are fleshed out by examples involving people. In other words, they are more likely to appreciate the practical outcome of theology or doctrine rather than the theology or doctrine itself.

The attributes of the Godhead to which they most easily respond are likely to be those aspects that enable them to enter into and to sustain a relationship with the Creator. They probably resonate more with such concepts as Redeemer, Saviour, Shepherd, Friend and, of course, Abba, Father, than to others such as Logos, Word or Truth. The latter are likely to be a real magnet for those of a more detached and logical outlook, the analytical people who are drawn first and foremost to loving God with their minds. For the more feeling-oriented people those names might initially have a rather chilling, impersonal quality about them that seems to create distance. They do not invoke the feeling of intimacy, and intimacy is what these people most seek in prayer. Some find their intimacy in liturgy, and some in extempore prayer, but intimacy is for them the heart of prayer. Even using the word 'heart' here is to use a feeling-oriented word.

Feeling people are likely to want an experience of God more than they want to know *about* Him. They yearn to draw rich meaning from the Giver of Life in a personally applicable way. They need to know God first in their hearts. They must feel that they have reached his heart and been touched by him, before they can begin to love him with their minds. It is of course important for them to progress to that also but for them it will follow from loving him with their hearts, it is not their initial response. Their spontaneous prayer is much more that of loving God with all the heart, and the 'all' is very important to them.

They are likely to relish many of the phrases found in passages such as The Song of Songs, 'I delight to sit in his shade . . . He has taken me to the banquet hall, and his banner over me is love' (2:3, 4). I well remember one time when I was feeling particularly alone in the world, that verse meant so much to me, and it has continued to do so. It was amazing how the sense of being personally escorted swept over me. Without ever leaving my chair I had the very real sense of being escorted in a very beautiful and caring and intimate way so that I was oblivious to all else. We were with each other, and at that moment nothing else mattered.

What did matter was the depth of the relationship and the engagement of my heart. The whole
feeling side of my nature, indeed all of my being,
was caught up in the reality of the experience.
It was a very real and a very deep experience
that taught me more about the love of God for
me personally than all the many sermons I had
listened to over the years. I learned a great truth
that for me was better apprehended through my
feelings than through my mind. Head knowledge left
me cold and unaffected. Heart knowledge changed
me.

Of course I would like all my times of prayer to
be as rich and as rewarding, but I fear that that
would be rather like desiring to live all the time
off chocolate biscuits! Such times are, for me at
least, the red letter days rather than the norm.
There is so much more to a prayer relationship
than the golden glow and the highlights. Often it
requires discipline for one who relies largely on
feelings, to press on in the absence of any particular feeling content, and seek God for himself
alone.

There is a particular danger here for people with
a personality bias towards feelings. They can all too
easily come to consider that they 'haven't prayed',
or at least that they have not 'prayed properly'
unless their feelings have been stirred in some way.
Feelings form such a large part of their lives that
quite naturally they also want to feel their prayer
(or the effect of their prayer). When anyone falls
into this trap they are forgetting that prayer is in
essence a matter of being wholly attentive to God,
no matter what the outcome. It can be hard for
feelers to grasp that when they remain unmoved

during prayer, and when they do not feel particularly engaged with God, they have still prayed. They do well to remind themselves that prayer most definitely (and mercifully) does not depend on feelings. They have prayed if they have disposed themselves towards God, holding themselves available to him by fixing their gaze on him rather than on their own preoccupations.

This is a very hard lesson that goes against the grain for them. They often have to exercise real discipline to stay on at prayer without the accustomed stimulus and the warmth of feelings to keep them attentive to God. Fortunately for most of us, we are not required to be successful, or productive, we are only expected to be faithful. The trouble is that so often we expect of ourselves something more than, or certainly something different from, that which God requires. We look for some sort of productivity, for something almost tangible, to result from our times of prayer. It is especially hard for the feelers who are also activists in attitude to remain receptive and open to God when nothing seems to be happening. They yearn for interaction, and they rely on feedback in any conversation. When these are absent they feel bereft and directionless.

If God chooses to reveal himself or his purposes in any way, or to move these people in their feelings, then that is great. They begin as it were to glow in this manifestation of his presence. But if for any reason, and especially if for no apparent reason, God does not choose to reveal himself, they will still have prayed. When 'nothing happens' or seems to happen during prayer because feelings have not been activated, then it is important for feelers to remind themselves that they have nevertheless still been at prayer.

The natural reaction at such times is generally to feel cheated, or short-changed in some way. What is most valued by them in life, what indeed they have come to rely on a great deal of the time, has been omitted from this most cherished of relationships. Some people are quite likely to feel guilty and to ask themselves where they have gone wrong, or when they have not been sufficiently attentive to God since they have not felt his presence. This of course is to confuse the gift with the Giver. They are seeking the gift of having their feelings stirred rather than concentrating on the Giver of gifts, irrespective of whether or not he gives gifts that day.

It is another hard discipline to learn, to seek him for himself alone, rather than for the gifts that he may, or may not, bring. So often we are like children at Christmas. We get excited by all the presents, the activity and the novelty, and then we tend to forget the reason for the gifts. We even tend to lose sight of the One who brings and distributes these gifts that have delighted us.

Those people who initially love God more with the heart than with the mind are likely to be stirred by the personal element in anything that they do or receive or read. For instance they are likely to be especially warmed when the elements are offered to them *by name* at communion, or when some cause dear to their hearts is specifically included in the vocalised intercessions during a church service. And they are likely to be particularly fond of Scripture passages that contain a personal element. For instance Isaiah in particular has a number of passages that speak about being known *by name* to God. Examples are 'Fear not, for I have redeemed you; I have called you by name, you are mine' (43:1 RSV), 'I summon [call] you by name and bestow on you a title of honour' (45:4), 'I will give them an everlasting name that will not be cut off' (56:5). 'You will be called by a new name . . . You will be a crown of splendour in the LORD's hand, a royal diadem in the hand of your God' (62:2,3).

They will always be especially drawn to passages that encourage and foster a personal, intimate relationship with a God who can be known personally. It is not enough for them to know the principles of the faith. They need to both know and experience how those principles can work out for them in a practical way. For instance, on the subject of guidance they will be glad to know that it is a person who guides them, and to read of this in such passages as 'Whether you turn to the right or to the left, your ears will hear a voice behind you, saying "This is the way; walk in it"' (Is 30:21).

They will also treasure passages that reassure them of their identity in God, and of their worth to him. An example of this is Isaiah 49:15–16;

'Can a mother forget the baby at her breast
    and have no compassion on the child she has
        borne?
Though she may forget,
    I will not forget you!
See, I have engraved you on the palms of my
    hands.'

And when the going gets tough they will want to be reminded that they are not left to cope on their own, for they do have the hand of a personal God to hold them. A passage that speaks of this theme, another great Isaiah one, is

'Do not fear, for I am with you;
  do not be dismayed, for I am your God.
I will strengthen you and help you;
  I will uphold you with my righteous right
    hand . . .
For I am the LORD, your God,
  who takes hold of your right hand.'

(Is 41:10,13)

Another characteristic of people with a bias towards the feeling aspects of life is that they tend to readily identify with people, whatever the circumstances. They are inclined to have very definite feelings about the characters in anything that they read or hear. They have a distinct tendency to sum up people or events in a subjective way, as ones that they themselves either like or dislike. They are very prone to become, as it were, part of the story itself, to jump into it and see things from the inside. It does not come naturally to them to remain as impartial outsiders.

The other outstanding feature of this group of people is that they have a great desire for harmony and peace. They value harmony *between* people, and it is also very important for them to be at peace *within* themselves. Any hint of disharmony is so disturbing to them that it can easily disrupt their concentration on other things. Frequently they have to stop what they are doing and attend to the matter that is disturbing them, if they possibly can, before resuming whatever activity was interrupted in this way. They really cannot function well, if at all, when they are at odds within themselves, or with others. This tendency can even be so strong that their efficiency may be lowered if they are in the presence of people who are at odds with each other, even if they are not personally involved in the disputed matter.

Recently I was taking a weekend on 'Discovering more ways into prayer' and we started by listing various aspects of prayer. We had several sheets of flipchart paper pinned to the walls and still no one had mentioned dealing with anger through prayer. It was as though uncomfortable emotions were unacceptable, and were therefore kept out of the prayer relationship. I had to work really hard to get anyone to admit that it is important to include the less presentable side of ourselves. We had quite a discussion about bringing the more 'negative' thoughts and feelings into our prayer.

For feelers, harmony is generally equated with goodness and desirability. Therein lies another prayer pitfall to which they may succumb. There is the danger that when they feel ill at ease during prayer they may decide that it is more comfortable not to pray at all. Some assume that since discomfort is, in their scheme of things, a 'bad' position to be in, then discomfort that arises during prayer must mean that the prayer itself is in some indefinable way 'bad' prayer.

Because of their natural tendency to want to return to a state of inner harmony, there is a strong temptation for them to move swiftly on, out of the discomfort zone. They want to feel more at peace again. Such a temptation generally needs to be resisted. It is likely that they will benefit more by remaining with their disquiet in order to find out what God may be trying to say to them about some matter. This is yet another hard discipline to learn, to hang in there until the possible reason for their unease begins to become clear.

Left to ourselves we are all too likely to repeat such mistakes, and to stay with our usual pattern of wanting to move on too soon. For this reason a trusted spiritual director or 'soul friend' can be most valuable. He or she will be well acquainted with such prayer traps and can be very useful in helping one to negotiate this and the other hazards already mentioned.

Having looked at the main features of a personality that is biased towards feelings, we can begin to understand the particular emphases that their prayer is likely to take. These features mean it will be distinct from the focussed prayer that comes more naturally to those with a bias towards the use of the senses. It also differs from the musing butterfly approach of intuitive imagination, and of those with a preference for logical analyses. We can begin to see some of the ways that the prayer of those who first and foremost tend to love God with all the heart is likely to differ from the ways of prayer we have looked at in preceding chapters.

Firstly this prayer is likely to be people-centred. People are the chief interest and the main focus of their lives, and so it is around people issues that they will pray most naturally most of the time. They tend to be the intercessors, and to be drawn towards intercessory prayer. The extravert feelers are likely to want to pray aloud in the company of others, They seldom have any difficulty in vocalising their intercessions and may find that their natural habitat is in prayer meetings. The introvert ones are more likely to be comfortable as solo intercessors, or perhaps when praying with one or two trusted friends who function as prayer twins or triplets. If they do attend larger prayer meetings they are likely to prefer to participate silently most of the time. They will probably simply stay away if there is too much pressure for 'everyone to take part and speak up'.

It is not only people that they value, but the relationship between people. More than that, they themselves want to remain in relationship with God and they are likely to understand him best in relational terms. They will resonate most with titles of the Godhead that denote a particular relationship. Father, Saviour, Comforter; Redeemer, Shepherd, Friend of sinners – all these will draw forth a ready response from feelers. Because forgiveness is necessary to retain a right relationship with God and with others, issues of forgiving and being forgiven are also likely to be a particular feature of their prayer.

Secondly, being feeling-oriented people, the feelings aroused by various encounters during the day, or by news items in the paper and on television, become the stuff of prayer for them. Because they value harmony and peace they will be moved whenever they hear of disharmony, illness, unkindness or personal trouble of any sort. They will work for harmony, and pray for it probably more than any other personality type.

When they use Scripture as a starting point for their prayer they are likely to dwell most frequently on passages capable of having a very personal application, like those already quoted in this chapter.

Alternatively they may choose to take a narrative, spending time to identify with several characters in turn. They might decide to be there, in the setting of the time, as one of the people written about. Some may prefer to remain as themselves but to be transported back in time and be looking on at the scene. They note each of their reactions and thoughts, and observe the responses of the people around them.

Whatever scripture they read they are likely to apply it first to themselves and to situations that they know. Only after doing so might they begin to search out the principles on which the story or the teaching is based. An example of how the chosen Bible reading method of those who love God first of all with the heart differs from that of those who love him first with their minds, and taking exactly the same passage, is used as a prayer exercise at the end of this chapter.

In order to develop a more rounded life of prayer, feelers will need to work at loving God with all their minds, as well as with all their hearts. One useful way to do this is to read a chosen portion of Scripture with the aid of a good commentary. Learn to really wrestle with God over the things that offend your feelings, or that you do not understand, instead of relying only on your feelings about them. Train yourself to look for the principle behind whatever you read, as well as its application for you personally. Try to make sure that you move on from your individual prayer into working out any implications it may have in your community, and in any wider application in society at large. Is God perhaps now calling you, through the arousal of some feeling in the matter, to go out and get involved in some issue of social concern?

Main Features of 'Heart' Prayer

- It is people-centred.
- It is characterised by an initial emotional response.
- It involves a relationship of heart more than of intellect.
- There is a greater stress on experiencing God than on knowing about him.
- There is a great desire for harmony and peace.
- God is most readily worshipped as Redeemer; Creator; Saviour; Shepherd; Abba, Father.

Points to Ponder

- Prayer does not depend on feelings.
- Learn to seek God for himself alone. Do not confuse the gift with the Giver.
- We are called to be faithful in prayer, not successful or productive.
- Prayer is being wholly attentive to God at any moment.

Pitfalls to Avoid

- Believing that feelings must be stirred for prayer to be valid.
- Seeking God for the blessings he may give, rather than for himself alone.
- Avoiding discomfort by moving on too soon, without waiting to learn what God may be wanting to say.

Prayer Exercise

1. Read the Gospel of John, chapter 13, verses 1–17.

   • Read it again, applying all of your senses. Let your imagination bring the scene and the people to life for you.
   • Recall a situation in your own life when you felt tired and footsore. Bring that situation to Jesus. Let him cleanse, refresh and restore you. Let yourself experience this process in detail.

     – What are you most aware of? What do you feel?

     – Hear him say to you by name 'Unless I wash you . . .'

     – Respond as seems right for you.

     – Hear him say 'Wash one another's feet, especially those of . . .' If you resist, talk to him about your resistance.

   • Before you leave, hear him bless you.

2. If you want to learn to respond to God as much with your mind as with your heart, then on another occasion take exactly the same passage. This time read it through and ask the following questions:

   • What does it mean to 'be clean'?
   • What, in today's society, would be the equivalent of washing someone's feet?
   • How can society/the church do this?
   • How can I 'wash the feet' of another?

- Who, specifically, does Jesus ask me to serve in this way?
- How can I best do so?
- When should I do it?

Ruth Faulkner. Spain. Jan 1993.

6

Lifestyle Implications

People tend to develop a more or less coherent and unifying lifestyle as a result of the personality characteristics that we have been looking at so far. Their lifestyle attitude will in turn affect the manner in which they are best able to nourish their spiritual lives, and the overall patterns of prayer that they tend to favour. It is also one of the influences that determines which forms of public worship they are apt to prefer.

Some people are renowned for being orderly and quick to make decisions. Structure and boundaries, tradition and the social conventions are generally important considerations for them. They like things to be predictable. These people generally thrive when life is settled, but they are prone to become anxious when they go through periods of transition and uncertainty. Not to be in control of their lives, and having arrangements left with loose ends, are likely to be sources of real stress for them.

They are most at ease when things are clearly decided and when life is stable. Leaving anything unsettled makes them uncomfortable, with the result that they have a tendency to make premature decisions. They are in danger of bringing matters to a conclusion before they have gathered all the facts that would enable them to make the best possible decision. In extreme cases they may take the line that almost any decision is better than leaving things up in the air. They can always make a decision to change a decision, if that can be proved to be really necessary. If there has been no clear decision in the first place then they just do not know where they are.

In their hurry to have things settled, to get on and reach a decision, they sometimes narrow down the opportunities that could be open to them. These are people who like to make their plans as well as their decisions quite explicit. Having made plans they are likely to stick to them as they stand, unless of course they make a fully conscious decision to make an alteration. They like to plan their work and other activities, and they are likely to follow their plans through until each task is completed.

Sometimes they can be so set on one particular goal that they may be unaware of changing circumstances. They may simply not notice that the situation has changed and now other tasks are actually more urgent. At times they may continue to follow their original plans when a change is really called for; what should heve been merely guidelines become set tram lines that confine their outlook. This restricts the possibilities they are prepared to consider.

The diary and filofax are likely to figure prominently in their lives. Often they have a strong work ethic which makes them concentrate so much on their goals that they can seem to lose the joy of simply being alive. I remember on one occasion observing a friend approach another in determined manner, large diary open and pen poised so that the other actually winced. Being of a different personality make-up, she probably felt trapped by the very action that gave security to the first one who wanted things pinned down.

For people with this decisive lifestyle there is almost always (some would like it to be absolutely always!) a right and a wrong way to do things. This includes the supposition that there is a right (and therefore a wrong) way to pray. Sometimes they can get so over-concerned about praying 'the right way' that they lose all ability to be spontaneous. They tend to continue with their usual approach and may be reluctant to branch out and try any new way. When they adhere too closely to their habitual ways and to their own plans there is the danger that they may become inflexible. In particular they may become reluctant to respond to the gentle nudging of the Holy Spirit when he wishes to lead them into a new avenue of thought or service.

God showed the best and the most creative of these decisive characteristics right at the foundation of the world, when he brought order out of chaos. All the way through the Old Testament he is revealed making decisions and choices, drawing up laws, defining boundaries and outlining proper conduct. It is this aspect of God that Solomon addressed in his prayer of dedication of the Temple, recorded for us in 1 Kings 8:23, when he repeatedly emphasised the total reliability of God. Recurrent phrases are 'You who keep your covenant . . .'; 'you have kept your promise . . .'; 'with your mouth you have promised and with your hand you have fulfilled it'. In a whole variety of situations that he foresaw he called on God to 'hear . . . forgive . . . restore; hear . . . forgive . . . teach; hear . . . forgive and act'.

Solomon knew his God to be predictable, stable and trustworthy.

Both Old and New Testaments emphasise that life is about decisions and choices. The great exposition of the Law recorded in Deuteronomy ends in chapter 30 with the words '. . . I have set before you life and death, blessings and curses. *Now choose life*, so that you and your children may live' (v 19, my italics). And the necessity to stick to that decision, once made, is in effect the cost of discipleship. It is echoed in the words of Jesus when he said 'No-one who puts his hand to the plough *and looks back* is fit for service in the kingdom of God' (Luke 9:62, my italics).

Jesus had a framework to his life, but he was never rigid and inflexible. We know he had his routine, for we are told that, 'He went to Nazareth, where he had been brought up, and on the Sabbath day he went into the synagogue, *as was his custom*' (Luke 4:16, my italics).

He certainly had his habitual practices but he never let them become restrictive. When challenged for allowing his disciples to pick ears of corn as they walked along on the Sabbath (symbolic of working), he retorted that 'the Sabbath was made for man, not man for the Sabbath' (Mark 2:27).

By contrast, other people develop a lifestyle which is quite different. It is likely to be marked more by adaptability, spontaneity, enjoyment and flexibility. They like to go with the flow of whatever life brings, preferring to do things rather more on the spur of the moment than by having pre-planned them. They want to discover what is going on in the world more than they want to control it. Generally they are more interested in finding out about life than they are in trying to pin it down in order to make it manageable, predictable and safe.

These people tend to be uncomfortable with too much structure in their lives. They consider that rules and regulations exist to be guidelines only, they tend not to see them as absolutes at all. They have a somewhat similar attitude towards decisions, believing that these are provisional rather than unalterable. There is always the chance that more information may come their way and that of course would require a modification of the original decision. They like to keep all their options open as long as they possibly can, and so they generally defer all decision-making as long as possible.

I get a lot of notices about meetings and other events, and I have no difficulty regarding those I definitely am or am not interested in pursuing. It is the in-between ones that cause the trouble. Often I inadvertently let the passage of time make the decision. Sometimes the leaflets to do with those things I am unsure about lie on a 'perhaps' or 'pending' pile. (I cannot even decide what to call that part of my filing system!) Every now and then when either I want something that is likely to be lurking there, or the 'deep litter filing system' has become too unwieldy, I go through it and thankfully throw away all those notices that are now out of date. Time has taken away the need (and the opportunity) to make a decision.

People with this flexible, wait and see lifestyle, enjoy variety in almost everything. They generally prefer randomness to routine, and are likely to resist attempts to pin them down. At times they can find tradition irksome, often having the urge to break the mould and branch out into something that they have not done before. They want to try everything in order that they might not miss anything.

In spiritual things, too, they want to keep their options open, and to try out most of the avenues that come to their attention. They are generally interested in a wide variety of approaches. They are likely to resist any attempt to pin them down to Bible reading or prayer schedules drawn up by others. They flourish most when they are free to follow their current interest. They enjoy variety and prefer to explore topics as they arise rather than when they appear in a schedule. The danger for them is that by following too many enticing pathways they may at times not be responsive when the Holy Spirit is wanting them to pay more attention to one particular area. They may disregard his restraining influence when he is urging them to stay still long enough for him to deal with a particular issue in their lives. That danger apart, when they have freedom to explore, and adequate variety to enrich them, they will grow when encouraged to do so in a way that is consistent with their personality.

These people are more likely to wilt than to flourish if an unalterable, fixed regime is advocated for them. Some, generally prevailed upon by mentors with decisive lifestyles, do take out yearly subscriptions to one or other of the various Bible reading schemes. Often they collect the prayer outlines promoted by numerous organisations, but tend to find them burdensome rather than helpful. Many do try to follow the schedules as recommended but they often only get part way and then find that their interest has waned. When this happens they are likely to presume there must be something wrong with them to lose interest like this. Some soldier on although the zest has gone, and sadly a number drop out altogether. Rather than pressing on as before they may need encouragement to try something a little different. They probably need to shop around and find an approach which does hold their interest and attention at this stage of their spiritual development – experimenting and exploring every means open to them. In the end they will probably cover the whole spectrum, but they do need to do it their own way and in their own time.

We see the flexible, perceptive character of God himself right from the first chapter of the Bible. After every act of creation he stopped, considered and 'saw that it was good' (Gen 1:3, 9, 12, 18, 21, 25). And when he did a review of all that he had made he found that 'it was very good' (Gen 1:31). His great flexibility also comes through in such accounts as Abraham pleading with him to save the city of Sodom. If even fifty righteous people can be found in the city it will be spared, for their sakes. Emboldened by this attitude Abraham goes on to bring the required number down to forty-five, forty, thirty, twenty and finally to just ten, and God graciously agrees each time (Gen 18:22–33).

That much mis-quoted character, Jonah, was actually angry with God for showing this same flexibility towards the people of Nineveh. They listened to the message he delivered to them, responded and turned from their evil ways, with the result that God 'had compassion and did not bring upon them the destruction he had threatened' (Jonah 3:10). Jonah grumbled, 'I knew that you are a gracious and compassionate God, slow to anger and abounding in love, a God who relents from sending calamity' (4:2). He seems to have felt that he was mocked because they listened to his message and therefore his predictions did not occur.

This attitude of God is especially echoed throughout the prophets. 'I am the LORD, who exercises kindness, justice and righteousness on earth, for in these I delight' (Jer 9:24). Ezekiel speaks on God's behalf, 'I myself will search for my sheep and look after them. As a shepherd looks after his scattered flock when he is with them, so will I look after my sheep. I will rescue them from all the places where they were scattered . . .' (Ezek 34:11–12). Through Hosea he says he 'will make the Valley of Achor [weeping] a door of hope' (Hosea 2:15). And so we could go on through all the prophets. The emphasis is on searching out in order to restore, to look after, to nourish and build his people up.

We find frequent emphases on change, and especially on things being made new. Psalms 40, 96, 98 and 149 all talk about singing a new song, something which always delights and appeals to the person with a flexible lifestyle. Jesus himself showed many of these flexible characteristics, just as when it was appropriate to do so, he also showed the more decisive ones. He was not bound by the social conventions of his day. Not only did he go through Samaria, but he actually asked a Samaritan woman for a drink of water although in his day the Jews had no dealings with the Samaritans (John 4:9). He touched people regarded as untouchable, notably those with leprosy (Luke 5:12) and even the dead (Luke 8:53). In his teaching he often stretched, and at times actually reversed, the established social order. He changed 'Love your neighbour and hate your enemy' into 'Love your enemies and pray for those who persecute you' (Matt 5:43).

When functioning at their best, people with an organised lifestyle are likely to make and maintain a systematic Bible reading plan, and to have a consistent pattern of prayer. If at all possible they generally like to have clearly worked out when and where they will pray, for how long and in what form. Some like to map out what the subject of their prayer, or at least of their intercessions, will be on different days of the week. Such a planned approach is seldom helpful long term for those with the more flexible lifestyle. They actually need variety and change to keep them on track, the very things that are likely to be unsettling and unhelpful to the organised people.

The vast majority of Bible reading notes and prayer plans that I have come across appear to me to be written by people with a decisive lifestyle. Most schemes seem designed to encourage everyone, regardless of personality, to adopt their particular method. There is a real need to encourage those with a flexible lifestyle to devise ways that are more suitable for their own particular requirements. The notes and plans that are written do not often take account of how necessary it is for a sizeable proportion of the population to be autonomous and spontaneous. People who value those things tend to embark on whatever scheme is recommended with initial enthusiasm and then to feel guilty when their interest wanes. They are likely to assume (and even to be taught) that the fault lies in themselves rather than in the method or material being advocated. Currently there is not much available for them.

One day, in my work of assessing people for fitness to serve overseas, I received a referral note which included the query 'Is he nourishing his spiritual life adequately?' I suspect that it was written by a personnel officer with an organised approach to prayer and spiritual matters as well as to life in the office and at home. The applicant just never would fit into that particular mould, for his gifts lay elsewhere. His life story showed that he was much more of an immediate response person, a trouble shooter and negotiator rather than a stabiliser and traditionalist. He was action oriented, living mainly through his senses and with a decidedly flexible lifestyle.

Such people resist being tied down in any way and it was clear to me that he was most unlikely to nourish his spiritual life in a traditional way as perhaps the personnel officer valued for herself. Talking this over with him it seemed that he could best be helped by arming himself with a number of short and varied studies such as can be found in some books, particularly those written for the Lent and Advent seasons. He and others like him might manage to complete about three-quarters of any one such study outline and then they would probably need to move on to something quite different in order to maintain their momentum. Sometimes they return to one of their unfinished study books at some later date, but mainly they prefer to move on. Being on the move is what energises them for service.

Points to Ponder

- A fixed routine that is helpful for some may be counter-productive for those with an opposite lifestyle.
- Bible reading plans and notes that help people

with a decisive lifestyle may not be sufficiently responsive to current interests for those with a flexible lifestyle.

Pitfalls to Avoid

For those with a DECISIVE LIFESTYLE.
* Making premature decisions on insufficient data.
* Allowing guidelines to become tram-lines.
* Letting the work ethic rob you of the joy of simply being alive.
* Being so set in your ways that you are unable to respond to a new leading of the Holy Spirit.

For those with a FLEXIBLE LIFESTYLE.
* Keeping options open so long you do not get around to making necessary decisions.
* Living in such an unstructured way that you never get around to reasonably regular reading of Scripture.
* Considering that since you pray 'at all times' you do not also need to have times when you specifically 'give yourself to prayer'.
* Following so many new paths that you do not stay on the one where the Holy Spirit wants to meet with you.

Some Helps for those with an Organised Lifestyle

* There are a number of schemes to encourage systematic and regular Scripture reading. Many people like to use the daily lectionary.

- A variety of Bible reading notes on which to focus your prayer can be obtained from Christian bookshops, notably those published by:
  – Scripture Union, Lion Publishing, Peter's Way, Sandy Lane West, Oxford OX4 5HG
  – Bible Reading Fellowship, Lion Publishing, Peter's Way, Sandy Lane West, Oxford, OX4 5HG
  – Crusade for World Revival, STL, PO Box 300, Kingstown Broadway, Carlisle CA3 0QS.

Some Helps for those with a flexible Lifestyle

- Browse around several Christian bookshops. Scan the advertisements in a number of religious magazines.
- Make your own choice. Ring the changes. Experiment.
- Enjoy yourself. Keep praying your way, and keep on praying.

Notes

Introduction
1. Mother Mary Clare, *Encountering the Depths* (London, DLT, 1981) p 8.

Chapter 1
1. Richard Foster, *Prayer* (London, Hodder & Stoughton, 1992) p 35.

Chapter 2
1. David Adam, *Power Lines, Celtic Prayers about Work* (London, Triangle, 1992).

Chapter 3
1. Bruce Duncan, *Pray Your Way* (London, DLT, 1993) p 107.
2. Ibid, p 110.
3. Ibid, p 111.
4. David Runcorn, *Space for God* (London, Daybreak, 1990) p 120.
5. C.S. Lewis, *Letters to Malcolm* (London, Fontana, 1966) p 7.

Chapter 4
1. C.S. Lewis, *The Four Loves* (London, Fontana, 1963).

The *Exploring Prayer* Series

Edited by JOYCE HUGGETT

Each book in the *Exploring Prayer* series uses
the author's hard-won experience to point the
reader to God – the One who listens and answers.
Authors have been encouraged to draw upon
their own Church tradition so that all can benefit
from the riches of the various strands of the
Church: catholic, evangelical and charismatic. The
photographs and illustrations in each book have
been chosen to reinforce the text.

Angela Ashwin
PATTERNS NOT PADLOCKS

Prayer for parents and all busy people, suggesting
practical ideas and initiatives for prayer building
on the chaotic, busy-ness of everyday life.

James Borst
COMING TO GOD

A stage by stage introduction to a variety of
ways of using times of stillness, quiet and
contemplative meditation.

Joyce Huggett
FINDING GOD IN THE FAST LANE

Encouragement and teaching on how to encounter
God and enjoy intimacy with him, despite the
demands of modern-day living.

The *Exploring Prayer* Series

EDITED BY JOYCE HUGGETT

Wendy Miller
SPIRITUAL FRIENDSHIP
How prayer and Bible meditation, journalling and attentive listening can be woven into relationships, thereby promoting mutual enrichment and re-invigorated prayer life

Michael Mitton
THE SOUNDS OF GOD
Helpful hints on hearing the voice of God, drawn from the contemplative, evangelical and charismatic traditions.

Gerald O'Mahony
FINDING THE STILL POINT
Writing from his own experience of severe mood swings, the author provides a means to understand and govern the movements of moods and feelings.

Joyce Rupp
PRAYING OUR GOODBYES
With the touch of a poet, Joyce Rupp has written about the times in our lives when we have to say goodbye: to a friend, a relationship, a job, etc.

Heather Ward
STREAMS IN DRY LAND
Praying when God is distant, when you feel bored or frustrated with your prayer life – or even empty, arid and deserted by God.